THE UNEXPECTED REVOLUTION

THE
UNEXPECTED REVOLUTION

Social Forces in the Hungarian Uprising

PAUL KECSKEMETI
THE RAND CORPORATION

STANFORD UNIVERSITY PRESS

STANFORD, CALIFORNIA

1961

Stanford University Press
Stanford, California

Library of Congress Catalog Card Number: 61-10927
Printed in the United States of America

PREFACE

The following study deals with the genesis of a revolutionary situation in Hungary, rather than with the revolutionary events themselves. Looking at the climax of October 23, 1956, one has the impression of a sudden jump from political stability to chaos. On closer inspection, however, it becomes apparent that the political situation had been in flux for a number of years before the final explosion. Indeed, in Hungary, as well as in the other countries of East Central Europe that passed into the Soviet orbit, political and social changes of the greatest moment had been compressed into a decade. The totalitarian rigidity of Stalinism was imposed upon these nations abruptly, almost without any period of transition. With Stalin gone, the inevitable relaxation of his system in the Soviet Union released a number of centrifugal, disruptive tendencies in the dependent territories. My purpose has been to show the interrelated social and political effects both of the forcible imposition of the Stalinist pattern and of its disintegration. Hungary, as an extreme case in both respects, offers particularly instructive evidence concerning the mechanism of the two processes.

For valuable criticisms and suggestions, I am indebted to Hans Speier, Joseph M. Goldsen, Herbert S. Dinerstein, Leon Gouré, and Myron Rush of The RAND Corporation, as well as to Robert C. Tucker of Indiana University, and to Henry L. Roberts, Alexander Dallin, and Paul Zinner of Columbia Uni-

Preface

versity. I should also like to express my thanks to Paul Ignotus, Thomas Aczél, Tibor Meray, George Pálóczi-Horváth, George Faludi, and George Heltai, whose accounts and analyses of the pre-revolutionary period, based upon their own experiences, were of inestimable help to me in my work.

This study was prepared as part of a continuing program of research undertaken by The RAND Corporation for the United States Air Force.

P. K.

CONTENTS

CONTENTS

THE UNEXPECTED REVOLUTION

1

INTRODUCTION

The Hungarian uprising of October 1956 was a dramatic, sudden explosion, apparently not organized beforehand by a revolutionary center; neither outsiders nor the participants themselves had anticipated anything like the irresistible revolutionary dynamism that would sweep the country. Not that premonitory signs of trouble to come were lacking. The Communist regime had visibly lost much of its authority and prestige. Its top leadership was publicly denounced and ridiculed in Party organs, and the Party leader himself, Mátyás Rákosi, was suddenly and somewhat mysteriously removed from his post in July. It was an open secret that the Party was torn by factional struggles and that once more, like three years before, a change of course was in the offing.

One can say in retrospect that the divisions within the Party's leadership, and the growing alienation of the regime's literary spokesmen, set the stage for the popular uprising that was to shake the Communist state to its foundations. Yet, up to the actual outbreak of the revolution, the stirrings of opposition and agitation for reform had very much the character of an internal family affair within the Party itself. Nothing indicated that the masses could, or would, take matters into their own hands. The upsurge of the anonymous mass as an active political force was a fantastic *coup de théâtre* which ended the regime's creeping internal crisis with a thunderclap and posed the problem of political change anew, in an infinitely more radical form.

Introduction

This sequence indicates that there were two separate processes contributing to political instability before the revolution,* one confined to strata within, or close to, the center of the Communist power apparatus itself, the other spreading throughout the broad, anonymous masses. These two processes will be called, for brevity's sake, the "elite" process and the "mass" process. The elite process was a gradual one. It manifested itself in various ways, ranging from personal and clique rivalries (found at all times in all Communist parties) to violent purges and their repercussions, and novel, exceptional forms of defiance from within the apparatus. In contrast to the gradual pattern of the elite process, the mass process took a discontinuous, jerky course: a long period of incubation, during which popular bitterness found practically no overt, public expression and was subdued even in its private manifestations, gave way abruptly to a period of total insubordination.

The revolution itself was the joint product of these two processes. One must assume that the incubation period of the masses would not have culminated in open insurrection if it had not been for the cumulative effect of the elite process steadily undermining the stability of the regime. In fact, repressed popular opposition had existed in every satellite country, but actual outbreaks occurred only where, as in Hungary, the Communist top elite became severely divided or disoriented. Nor would quarrels within the Communist political elite have led to a collapse of the regime if the masses had not entered upon the scene. Factional struggles as such involve only a regrouping within the political elite; the final result of this may be, and

* If the term revolution is used exclusively to designate a radical political overturn giving rise to a new regime, and precluding the restoration of the old, the events of October 1956 in Hungary cannot be called a revolution but merely a revolt. It should be noted, however, that the Communist regime would have been eliminated for good if it had not been for Soviet military intervention. Therefore, if only internal political forces are taken into account, October 1956 was a revolution.

2

often has been, a stronger, more complete control being exercised by the Party than before. Admittedly, in the pre-revolutionary period, the struggle within the elite involved not only personal and factional rivalries but also matters of principle: Rákosi's opponents in 1956 were calling for moral regeneration and a drastic reform of antipopular governmental practices. Their aim, however, was not to destroy the regime but to make it accepted and popular. It was only the dynamism of the masses which pushed events beyond mere reform from within.

In the following pages, an attempt will be made to show the interrelation between the elite pattern and the mass pattern of pre-revolutionary events. The mass pattern cannot be treated in detail, since it has left no articulate record of its development. It can only be tentatively reconstructed from the few brief instances of open opposition manifested by the masses and from interviews with ordinary people who had gone through the experience of Communist rule and its dramatic crisis in the revolution. Throughout the discussion, the emphasis will be on the *direction* of the events toward the revolutionary climax, and upon the mutually reinforcing effect the two processes had upon each other.

The division within the elite, however, has left ample record, and its history will be traced from the end of World War II and the emergence of Soviet-directed Communism as a major political force in Hungary. Chapter 2 introduces the most important elements confronting one another within the Party— the indigenous underground on the one hand, and the cadres returning from exile in Soviet Russia on the other. It will be shown that neither group was an autonomous agent; the balance of power was held throughout by the supreme Party authorities in Moscow to which all local Communists had to look for support in their maneuvers.

But the image of a three-person game, with two local contenders and an outside arbiter, does not give a true idea of the complexities of the situation. None of the principal groups in the drama had complete solidarity even within itself: there were personal rivalries and differences in outlook both within the main local groupings of Communists and within the Moscow leadership. Nor was the Party operating as a self-contained unit. As in all the Soviet-controlled or Soviet-manipulated countries of what was to become the satellite empire, the Communists were engaged in the grim business of imposing totalitarian control upon a recalcitrant society, using terror both to intimidate opponents and "class enemies" and to split, demoralize, and finally assimilate temporary allies. In the present context, however, attention will be directed mainly to those political trends and events in the Party that in one way or another contributed to the eventual disintegration of the Communist power structure. Chief among these were the mass purges of 1949 and the following years; the Communist state's all-out drive toward industrialization and the collectivization of agriculture; and, finally, the bankruptcy of this drive and the attempts of the post-Stalin regime in Moscow to repair the damage by policies of retreat and relaxation.

Chapter 3 deals with the first of these retreats, the New Course initiated by Stalin's successors. The relaxation dictated by Moscow occurred in smooth and gradual fashion in most of the satellite countries; but in Hungary it involved a highly dramatized revamping of basic policies and a change of government, Imre Nagy, a critic of collectivization and forced industrialization, being named Premier.[1] The regime never fully recovered from this abrupt change. The main policies of the New Course—concessions to the peasantry, relaxation of terror, and the shift of emphasis from industrialization to satisfaction of consumers' needs—might have had a soothing effect, had those responsible for the old, ruthless course been removed from the political scene altogether. Rákosi and his clique, however,

---

[1] Numbered notes will be found at the back of the book, pp. 161–67.

retained control of the Party and used their power to sabotage the New Course and undermine Nagy's position. The regime was thus prevented from reaping the potential benefits of relaxation while it did suffer from its disruptive effects. The easing of police terror encouraged active opposition to the system within the agricultural masses, as well as insubordination within the Party apparatus. What caused the most serious breach in the Party was the fact that the New Course put on its agenda the highly sensitive matter of Rákosi's terror against Party members. Moscow had insisted on this, without considering the political dangers inherent in opening up a moral chasm between the top Party leadership and the lower echelons.

One of the main themes of the present study, the political significance of irreconcilable moral conflicts within the Communist elite, will be taken up in Chapter 4, which deals with the revolt of the Communist intellectuals. As has already been mentioned, the mainsprings of this literary opposition were primarily moral ones. Chapter 5 shows how a second wave of relaxation of control, the "thaw" signalized by the Twentieth Congress of the CPSU in February 1956, opened more public channels for the intellectuals' opposition, and how the resulting ferment undermined the authority of the regime.

The Communist writers, in attacking the top leadership, hoped to gain a point of contact with the masses. Previously, they had extolled Communism for having freed the workers and peasants from capitalist and feudal oppression. Now they realized, to their mortification, that the people themselves had a different view of the situation, and that the workers and peasants, though by no means anxious to restore the *ancien régime*, felt thoroughly alienated from the new system. The writers hoped to get a sympathetic response by acknowledging their error and holding out hopes for redress. The masses, however, remained reserved and noncommittal. Indeed, one of the characteristic features of the pre-revolutionary incubation period was the contrast between the sullen silence maintained by the bulk of the people (peasants and industrial workers) and the intelligentsia's considerable propensity for self-expression. This is examined in Chapter 6.

The silence of the masses was, of course, a direct result of the control apparatus of the regime. This was not only a matter of police terror. Chapter 7 shows how the various new institutional environments created by the Communists enabled the regime to use a variety of economic and administrative techniques, in addition to propaganda and terror, to ensure discipline and subordination. Among the peasantry, passive resistance could not be stamped out completely; but, by and large, the masses maintained outward conformity. There was no way of telling how deep or widespread a disaffection existed among them. Indeed, such was the success of the Communist control apparatus that most of the people, left to themselves, had no awareness of any deep current of feeling potentially uniting them.

Perhaps the most extraordinary aspect of the Hungarian revolution was the rapidity with which a national consensus crystallized after the outbreak. This is the main topic treated in Chapter 8, which deals with the revolution itself. It is shown here how the mass pattern of revolution, latent until street fighting began, suddenly took over from the elite pattern, rendering all debates about internal reform of the system irrelevant. The people themselves, noncommittal and voiceless beforehand, defined the issue unambiguously as that of national liberation. Opposition to Russian occupation had been the hidden current which, unknown to the people, had created a unity of feeling among them.

Discussion of both the elite and the mass pattern is largely based upon interviews with Hungarians who lived through the pre-revolutionary period and the revolution, and subsequently escaped to the West. Between December 1956 and August 1957, I interviewed thirty-seven Hungarian refugees; twenty-five of these interviews were held between December 1956 and July 1957 in the United States (in New York, New Haven, and Washington), and twelve (with Hungarians who had fled after the revolution) took place in July and August 1957 in Europe (in London, Paris, Brussels, and Feldafing in Bavaria). Those interviewed in the United States belonged to all walks of life; they included peasants, workers, intellectuals, army officers, and anti-Communist political figures. The European group of respondents consisted of Hungarian intellectuals of various backgrounds, notably some ex-Communist writers who had been active in the Party opposition prior to the revolution. I also examined transcripts of over a hundred interviews collected in the Columbia University Project on the Hungarian Revolution.

Interviews of this kind raise many problems of bias, credibility, and representativeness. To begin with, the political opinions expressed in the interviews were particularly subject to "interviewer's bias," a tendency to say those things that would create a favorable impression. This bias may also have colored factual statements about the respondent's own role and about conditions in general; and further distortion may have resulted from incomplete knowledge, uncritical reasoning, and many other factors. Finally, the refugees did not represent a random sample of the Hungarian population, so that it would have been improper to impute any distribution of attitudes found among them to the population as a whole.

I have tried to eliminate errors due to these factors as best I could. In order to reduce "interviewer's bias," interviews were arranged on a personal basis, so as not to give them a character of official or officially sponsored interrogation. Moreover, direct questioning about political attitudes and beliefs was avoided. Instead, the respondents were encouraged to reminisce about personal experiences. The analysis was based upon spontaneously produced biographical material, rather than, say, upon the respondents' political value judgments. This type of material, contained both in my own interviews and in those of the Columbia Project, suggested certain patterns of experience apparently typical of various social groups (industrial workers, white-collar employees, peasants, intellectuals, and young people).

As regards these broad, characteristic patterns of experience, I treated the respondents as indeed representative of their respective social groups. There is, in fact, no reason to assume that the refugees as a group were atypical in these respects. Although the self-selection of the refugees clearly did lead to over- and underrepresentation of many sociological and attitude variables (occupation, religion, party affiliation, and so on), one still could not say that the respondents included a large number of marginal or deviant elements within their own social groups. As regards their major life experiences, they were just ordinary people. Hence, their reminiscences could be used to reconstruct, tentatively and in broad outline, the various processes that were going on at different social levels and that culminated in the October Revolution.

In Chapter 9, events in Hungary are compared with analogous processes observed elsewhere in the satellite area, notably East Germany and Poland. A concluding chapter, based upon the case material previously presented, draws some tentative general conclusions about factors of political instability inherent in Communist regimes.

2

FROM COALITION

TO PURGE

The entry of Soviet troops into Hungary in the autumn of 1944 made the Hungarian Communist Party virtually the decisive political power in the country. The existing state apparatus collapsed; there was a complete political vacuum. Small as the Communist Party was, it could have proclaimed the "dictatorship of the proletariat," had this been the Soviet government's policy at that time. Moscow, however, had different plans. It discouraged the immediate establishment of Soviet-type one-party governments in the countries from which the Germans had been driven by the Russian armies. Instead, the Soviets insisted upon organizing civil government in the liberated countries on a multi-party basis. The Communists were to participate in these governments alongside non-Communist (Social Democratic and even bourgeois) parties certified as "antifascist" by the occupation authorities.

The Soviet government's reasons for preferring this coalition blueprint to the immediate introduction of the Communist one-party state in the liberated territories cannot be detailed here. One of the reasons certainly was that Stalin was anxious not to antagonize the Western Allies as long as strong American and British armies were deployed on European soil; in addition, he probably was moved by other considerations, such as the need for the quick resumption of economic activities. In any case,

9

the coalition system as conceived by Moscow, although superficially similar to parliamentary democracy, departed from it in one essential respect. Unlike parliamentary coalitions of the normal kind, the "antifascist" coalitions of this new type were meant to be permanent and unchangeable in composition. This assured the Communists of unchallengeable tenure in all positions they had pre-empted, such as the ministries controlling the police and the courts. If and when they decided to use their power against their coalition partners, these partners would have no means of recourse. The "antifascist" coalition blueprint was so contrived that only the Communists could gain power within the coalition at their partners' expense. Thus, it was an effective device by which to prepare the ground for a delayed seizure of exclusive power by the Communist Party. No political grouping could hope to stave off this development indefinitely, what with the Communist Party enjoying the full support of Soviet military might, police power, and economic dominance. We shall see later by what methods the Hungarian Communists hollowed out the coalition system set up under the auspices of the Soviet military government.

The Communist Underground

The first step after liberation, however, was to form an "antifascist" coalition government, with the Communists in the beginning merely playing the role of junior partners. In Hungary, even this first step was difficult, for the country had no indigenous Communist movement to speak of. Not only had the Hungarian Communist Party been illegal since 1919; it was particularly impotent even as illegal parties go, because the short-lived Hungarian Soviet Republic of 1919 had left unhappy memories in all social classes. Elsewhere in Europe, Communist agitation, open or clandestine, could play upon the expectations of the dissatisfied, unencumbered by any Communist governmental record; in Hungary, however, there was

10

the memory of Béla Kun's regime to live down, a memory hateful to the peasantry and the middle strata and far from endearing even to the industrial workers. Thus, between the two world wars, the Hungarian Communist Party was a head without a body. A handful of leaders who had escaped to the Soviet Union after the debacle of 1919 constituted themselves as the Hungarian branch of the Third International; apart from this nucleus in exile, there was practically nothing. And even this nucleus was torn by factional differences.[1]

The Hungarian Communist leadership in exile repeatedly tried to set up a clandestine organizational network in Hungary during the twenties. Mátyás Rákosi, then a second-string member of the *émigré* group, returned to Hungary on such a mission in 1925; he was promptly arrested by the police, who had infiltrated the circle of conspirators with whom he was in contact. Two years later, the same thing happened to another emissary from Moscow, Zoltán Szántó.[2] Rákosi remained in prison in Hungary until 1940; thus he escaped Stalin's purges of the thirties in which Béla Kun, the head of the Communist leadership in exile, was liquidated. In 1940, when the Nazi-Soviet pact was in force, the Hungarian government, which followed Germany's lead in everything, pardoned Rákosi and allowed him to return to Russia. From then on, the leadership of the decimated Hungarian group in exile fell to Rákosi. During his absence, however, the Communists' efforts to revive the movement within Hungary had made no appreciable progress.

In the 1920's, there were a few crypto-Communists in the country among intellectuals and in the trade union movement, which was officially aligned with the Social Democratic Party. These, however, were mostly isolated individuals, and they made no attempt to organize a Communist underground. It was not until the thirties that Communist organizational activities got under way and then only on a very small scale. These stirrings had no proletarian class character. The left-

11

wing radicalism of the thirties was largely confined to the students. Communist cells came into being at the universities of Budapest and Debrecen; left-wing radicalism also had support among the faculty and pupils of the Györffy Colleges, educational institutions for young people of lower-class background. The students who became attracted to Communism in the thirties were idealists who saw Communism chiefly as a counterforce to fascism and Nazism. This attitude was characteristic of the period of the Popular Front, when Communism gained many sympathizers throughout the Western world by preaching the sacred union of all men of good will against the Nazi menace. In Hungary, this appeal was effective only among a few university students, although after the outbreak of war, these student conspirators of the thirties did gain a few recruits from their own generation, including some graduates of the General Staff College. This circle represented practically the only organized indigenous contingent the Party had when the Soviet army arrived.

The most prominent member of the indigenous network was László Rajk, who in 1932 had organized a Communist cell at the Eötvös College, a training center for the most highly qualified students in the Faculty of Letters at the University of Budapest. After serving a term in prison, Rajk became a professional revolutionary; he fought in the Spanish Civil War, was interned in France, and returned to Hungary during the war. His group also included Géza Losonczy, Julius Kállai, and Ferenc Donáth, former students at the University of Debrecen.

Isolated and insignificant at first, the indigenous Party organization began to move toward the center of political life during the war. Like other Communist parties, the Hungarian Communists abandoned all revolutionary and anticapitalist propaganda once the USSR was in the war, concentrating their efforts upon combatting the Axis. The Hungarian Communist

Party changed its name to "Peace Party" and offered to co-operate with the democratic parties of the opposition on an antiwar and anti-Nazi platform. Such a bloc did, in fact, come into being in March 1944, after the occupation of Hungary by German troops. The democratic opposition went underground and established the Hungarian Independence Front, in which the Communists were represented by Rajk and his circle. The Front also maintained liaison with high military circles around the Regent, Horthy, who was desperately anxious to quit the Axis before its defeat was consummated.

The non-Communist opposition parties adhering to the Front (Smallholders, Social Democrats, and Peasants) had both some popular following and functioning organizations; the Communists still lacked both. When one of the members of the Front, the Peasant Party leader Imre Kovács, met the Communist Party representative Ferenc Donáth for the first time, he asked him how many members the party had. The answer was: "We do not know, and it doesn't matter. We want to move the masses, and all we need for that is good leadership and well-trained cadres."[3] On the other hand, the Communists already had great prestige, since they were able to claim the backing of the Soviet Union, whose awesome shadow had begun to fall over the country. This enabled them to speak as equals, or even secret superiors, to the generals and well-established political figures with whom they were thrown together in the clandestine antiwar movement.

The "Muscovites" and the Indigenous Underground

With the entry of Soviet troops into Hungary, the moment had come for the Communists to launch political and organizational activity in the open and on a grand scale. This had to be done from scratch, since, as we have seen, the Party had only a leadership but no masses; or rather, it had two separate groups of leaders—Rákosi and his circle of *émigrés* on the one hand, and Rajk with his fellow conspirators on the other. From the first moment, there could be no doubt about which group held the real power. The group returning from Moscow—Rákosi, Ernö Gerö, Mihály Farkas, József Révai, Zoltán Vass, and a few others—constituted the elite and treated the indigenous contingent with contempt. At Debrecen, where the first post-liberation government of Hungary was set up in December 1944 under the watchful eye of the Soviet military authorities, the Communists of the Hungarian underground met the Moscow group for the first time. The encounter was anything but cordial. "Ferenc Donáth and Julius Kállai," recounts the Peasant Party leader Imre Kovács, "cut a very small figure at Debrecen." The "Muscovites" heaped abuse upon the indigenous group and told them off in biting fashion. Eventually, the indigenous functionaries were given positions within the Party hierarchy, but Donáth said bitterly that all the decisions were being made by the men at the top.[4]

The Moscow group indeed reserved all top positions for themselves. The first Politburo of the reconstituted Hungarian Communist Party, appointed in January 1945, contained no member of the domestic underground. It was not until a few months later, in May, that Rajk, returning to Hungary from a German concentration camp, was co-opted as a member.[5] The other civilian leaders of the former underground Communist Party (Losonczy, Kállai, and Donáth) had to content themselves with less important positions.

Because of the lack of trained cadres, the domestic underground could not be ignored altogether; the Muscovite *émigré* group was barely large enough to fill the top posts. The domestic Communists, however, had formidable competitors in a third group: Hungarian prisoners of war who had been recruited for the Party and received political training in captivity. The rise of the ex-prisoners within the Party hierarchy was assured, because the Russians had more confidence in them

14

than in the underground. It was in this way that unknown figures such as István Kossa and Antal Apró, who had played no political role previously, suddenly emerged into leading positions in the winter of 1944–45.

The underground, however, was strongly represented in the extralegal, terroristic apparatus of the Party. George Pálfy-Oesterreicher, a former general staff candidate active in the underground, and a few of his close associates rose behind the scenes to controlling positions within the reconstituted nucleus of the Hungarian military establishment, and built up an undercover military police force. This duplicated, and competed with, the political police headed by Gábor Péter, who also came from the underground.

Since major policy was dictated by Stalin, the heterogeneous elements from which the Hungarian Communist leadership was hurriedly patched together cooperated smoothly enough to all outward appearances. Whatever their previous ambitions may have been, Rajk and the former underground bowed to the authority of Rákosi and went along with the coalition policy endorsed by Moscow. The policy imposed extraordinary constraints upon the Communist Party at the beginning: in the first coalition government, formed in Debrecen in December 1944 and headed by General Béla Dálnoki Miklós, the Communists had only three portfolios. Of these, the most important was that of Agriculture, held by Imre Nagy, a Communist returned from Moscow who, however, did not belong to Rákosi's coterie.

Possession of the Ministry of Agriculture was essential to the Communists for reasons of political strategy: they counted upon winning a mass following among the peasantry by taking credit for a radical land reform, parceling out Hungary's big landed estates among the landless.[6] It was only after the completion of the land reform, in September 1945, that Nagy was given the portfolio of the Interior, the first cabinet post of key importance to be taken over by a Communist. This position, which carried with it control over the political police, became a very significant one toward the end of 1946, when the Communists began their drive against their coalition partners. At that time, the moderate Nagy was replaced as Minister of the Interior by the former underground leader Rajk, a far more ruthless and fanatical man.

The transition from the coalition regime to the Communist single-party state was not a smooth process. The elements involved in the transition were so heterogeneous that the unity of the Hungarian Communist Party was severely strained. The former underground, in particular, had been anxious for a quick showdown with the "reactionaries," that is, the non-Communist coalition partners. When the offensive against the latter began, the influence of the radicals, notably Rajk, inevitably increased. Within Rákosi's Muscovite group, there were the usual personal jealousies and rivalries. Thus, the transition was full of dangers for Rákosi.

Taking his cue from Moscow, Rákosi sought to conduct the Communist political offensive against the "reactionaries" at a slow, deliberate pace. His rivals and opponents in the Party were also looking to Moscow, hoping to take advantage of any signal favoring acceleration of the tempo. At that time, Tito was the outstanding exponent of the radical course, and the question was whether Stalin, who previously had been irked by Tito's extremism, would now give him his approval. In the end, the break between Tito and the Cominform enabled Rákosi to get the better of his rivals and destroy his chief radical opponent, László Rajk.

Rajk, who had spearheaded the offensive for dismantling the coalition regime, himself became a victim of the totalitarian police state he had helped to set up. The totalitarian regime buttressed by terror was inaugurated under Rákosi's auspices. The terroristic methods by which Rákosi imposed his law, however, contained the germs of his later downfall.

From Coalition to Purge

Terror Against the Coalition Partners

Only a very brief description of the terroristic actions directed against the non-Communist coalition parties can be given here.[7] Two main methods were used for this purpose: the discovery of antidemocratic conspiracies and the forced merger.

Between the end of 1946 and May 1947, most of the important Smallholders leaders were arrested on charges of plotting to overthrow the democratic republic, charges for which evidence was manufactured by the police. This left the leadership of the Smallholders Party in the hands of people totally subservient to the Communists; some independent-minded members left and formed their own parties, but these were eventually dissolved or forced to disband. By this method, the Smallholders Party, which in the elections of November 1945 had polled 57 per cent of the vote, was virtually eliminated.

The method of the forced merger had as its objective the termination of the independent existence of the Social Democratic Party. Terroristic pressure forced the party to expel those of its leaders who, rejecting the Communist slogan of "proletarian unity," held out for continued independence. The remainder, intimidated or won over by promises, voted the merger with the Communist Party at the "unification congress" of June 1948.

Thus, thanks largely to Rajk's ruthless energy as a terrorist, the Communists eliminated their two main rivals. However, once this was accomplished (with the capture of the Social Democrats), Rajk's career began to decline. In August 1948, he was forced out of the Ministry of the Interior (thus losing his police powers) and was made Foreign Minister instead.

The only thing that remained to be done to make the one-party regime an accomplished fact was to hold elections with a single list of candidates. As Secretary General of the "People's Front of Independence," an organization set up by the government to conduct propaganda for the single-list elections, Rajk

17

played his last important role. The elections took place in May 1949, with predictable success (94 per cent voting for the single list). Immediately afterward, Rákosi, no longer in need of Rajk's services, got rid of him in the most brutal fashion.

The Intra-Party Purge

Rajk was expelled from the Party on June 16, 1949, together with a close associate, Tibor Szönyi; their arrest was announced on June 19. In September, Rajk was tried on trumped-up charges of being an imperialist agent plotting with Tito to overthrow the Hungarian Communist regime. The prosecution also maintained that Rajk had been a fascist police spy before the war. Rajk admitted all the charges. He was sentenced to death, and his execution by hanging followed in October.

Rajk's execution was the signal for a succession of massive purges in which virtually the entire indigenous element in the Party was liquidated. The military members of the underground Communist Party, Generals Pálfy-Oesterreicher, Illy, and Sólyom, were executed; the civilian leaders mentioned above (Losonczy, Donáth, and Kállai) were sent to prison in 1951. The total number of purge victims has been estimated at 200,000.[8]

In the developments just outlined we can thus distinguish three consecutive stages: the coalition period, the anticoalition offensive of the Communist Party, and, finally, the purge of the Party itself. Events followed the same basic pattern in all satellite countries, with some differences in detail. Hungary's coalition period, for example, was second only to that of Czechoslovakia in the degree to which it approximated normal parliamentary democracy; Hungary's intra-Party purge, on the other hand, was the earliest in date and the most vicious of all satellite intra-Party purges.

The wave of terror that engulfed Hungary was directed against "class enemies" and opponents of Communism as well as against Communists and fellow-travelers. In our present context, however, we are concerned only with the intra-Party purge, directed against old Party members, and with the nature of the internal division within the Communist elite which led to the purge.

In all the satellite countries, the Communist purge victims came from the ranks of the indigenous Party; that is, from the apparatus that had existed prior to the entry of the Soviet troops. Those who had spent some time in the West during the war were particularly suspect. The organizers of the purges, on the other hand, were Muscovites. Now the question is, why did the latter element turn against the former with such destructive fury? Specifically, in Hungary, why did Rákosi liquidate Rajk and the indigenous underground Party?

THE LEFT OPPOSITION

Opposition, Rivalry, or Loyalty?

In the absence of complete data about the internal politics of the Hungarian Communist Party between 1944 and 1949, many conjectures are possible as regards the real reasons for the destruction of the indigenous underground in the purges of 1949–51. These conjectures may be reduced to three principal hypotheses:

(1) *The "opposition" hypothesis.*—The indigenous underground, led by Rajk, represented a real opposition within the Party. It disagreed with the Muscovite leadership group around Rákosi on questions of correct Party strategy and tactics, and possibly also on fundamental doctrine. According to an extreme version of this hypothesis, Rajk and his circle stood for "national" Communism, just as Tito did in Yugoslavia. Rajk, though a Communist, was a champion of Hungarian independence and had the support of the indigenous Party on this fundamental issue, whereas Rákosi and the former *émigrés* advocated total subservience to Russia. This was the real reason why Rajk had to perish. The orthodox Party line in Rákosi's

19

heyday also reflected the opposition hypothesis, but with a different accent: according to the official line, Rajk was not a hero but a villain, an agent of the imperialists.

(2) *The "rivalry" hypothesis.*—There were differences between Rajk and Rákosi regarding Party tactics and strategy, and possibly even on more fundamental matters, but these were not important enough to provoke a total break. Rákosi did not destroy the underground Party because of strategic, tactical, or ideological differences; his real reason for eliminating Rajk was that Rajk was a dangerous rival. As long as he was alive and commanded the support of a potential Party apparatus, Rákosi and the official apparatus controlled by him could not feel secure.

(3) *The "loyalty" hypothesis.*—Rákosi may have suspected Rajk of aspiring to the top position in the Hungarian Communist Party and plotting against him, but if so, Rákosi's suspicions were groundless. Rajk was actually a loyal, disciplined Communist for whom subordination to the official leadership was second nature. The same was true of the other Communist victims of the great purges. Thus, the purges were in fact gratuitous. If not from paranoid mistrust, Rákosi may have resorted to them from calculation. Wholesale terror, he knew, could help him to bolster his position in several ways. For one thing, it would ensure total, unquestioning obedience in the Party; for another, it enabled him to claim credit in Moscow for his vigilance in uncovering and eliminating vast numbers of Titoist traitors. Whatever Rákosi's true motive may have been, if there was any significant division in the Party's ranks it was brought about by the Communist authorities themselves, who created victims for no valid reason.

Which of these hypotheses is borne out by the facts? As we shall see, none of the three by itself provides a full explanation of the purge of the indigenous underground apparatus. Only a combination of elements from all three hypotheses can account for the purge policy.

From Coalition to Purge

The Official Line

With respect to the opposition hypothesis, the Communist official line has fluctuated wildly. Up to June 1949, no division in the ranks of the Hungarian Communist Party was officially admitted or even hinted at; Rajk, although somewhat diminished in status in 1948, was nonetheless a member of the Party aristocracy holding important Party and government offices. During the purge period, the regime asserted an extreme version of the opposition hypothesis: Rajk as well as the other Communist purge victims had been wreckers, plotting against the Party from within throughout their careers. During the "thaw" period, beginning in June 1953, a new line appeared, according to which disregard for "socialist legality" and misuse of police power had been responsible for the unjust persecution and imprisonment of many perfectly innocent and loyal comrades. Under great pressure, Rákosi himself admitted, in March 1956, that Rajk had belonged to this category, and that indeed *all* Communists or fellow-travelers liquidated or imprisoned in the purges were the innocent victims of a vicious police apparatus. This, the last official line of the pre-revolutionary regime (a line that survived the October Revolution) was an extreme version of the loyalty hypothesis.

The version of the opposition hypothesis asserted by the regime during the purge period was definitely gratuitous. The evidence against Rajk and his associates was palpably made of whole cloth.[9] It is safe to assume that the other purge victims, together with the non-Communists persecuted by the terror apparatus of the regime, were equally guiltless of the charges against them. My interviews with a number of such victims, whether opponents or (at the time of their arrest) supporters of the regime, strongly point to the conclusion that police and prosecution systematically used fictitious charges to destroy the accused, never mentioning the real reason why the regime wanted to be rid of them. A member of the Smallholders Party, for example, may have made himself obnoxious because he used

21

his authority to prevent Communist infiltration of his office; such a man was likely to be accused of plotting to overthrow the democratic republic. In other cases, the Communists decided that left-wing intellectuals of a Western frame of mind could never fit into the Communist order, even if they rallied to the Party; these were likely to be presented as Western agents and spies.[10] The same technique was used against Rajk. He was clearly innocent of the blatant crimes attributed to him, but the question is, what actual grievance did Rákosi have against him? Was Rajk the center of an inner opposition aligned against Rákosi on matters of policy?

The Indigenous Communists as a Left Opposition

There has been some speculation that Rajk represented a relatively liberal or democratic tendency within the Hungarian Communist Party, and that he fell out with Rákosi when Rákosi ended the multi-party coalition regime that had been in power from 1945 till 1949 and replaced it with a Communist one-party government.[11] This, however, is pure fantasy. Rajk and the indigenous Communists had no fondness for the democratic coalition. They had cooperated with non-Communist parties in the underground, but always with the thought that, after the entry of the Soviet troops, they would run the whole show. They were shocked, therefore, to learn from Moscow's mouthpiece, Rákosi, that for the time being they were expected to share power with "reactionaries" like the Smallholders and "traitors" like the Social Democrats. They remonstrated with Rákosi for imposing this indignity upon them, a point on which we have Rákosi's own testimony. At the zenith of his career, on February 29, 1952, Rákosi delivered a speech to the Communist Party Academy in Budapest in which he reminisced about the early post-liberation period:

> At the beginning of 1945, when our country was liberated and after 25 years of underground activity the Hungarian

Communist Party was able to enter the political arena legally and openly, we soon realized that the majority of our Communists did not understand the strategy and tactics of our Party. . . . The greater part of those comrades who were not acquainted with or did not understand our strategical plan devised during the war, were surprised at such a broad coalition, composed of heterogeneous elements, and treated it often with antagonism. How often during those weeks were we reproached by good comrades: "This is not what we expected of you." And they told us what they wanted. ". . . Now that the Red Army has liberated us—let us profit by this opportunity to restore the proletarian dictatorship."[12]

Rákosi made no explicit reference in this connection to Rajk and his associates in the wartime underground; he only spoke about anonymous "good comrades" who criticized him and his coalition policy. He had, however, good reasons for glossing over the real nature of the split that existed in the Party in the immediate post-liberation period. It was not expedient in 1952 to recall the role that Rajk and other purge victims had played in the indigenous underground, nor was it politic to admit that Rajk had been pressing for the immediate establishment of the one-party state; for, according to the official theory, Rajk had been nothing but a Western agent and fascist police spy. Still, to those acquainted with the record it was clear that "the majority of our Communists" could only be members of the wartime Rajk apparatus, since there were no other indigenous Communists at the time of liberation. Rákosi's account, veiled but certainly accurate as far as it goes, leaves no doubt that the coalition policy created a sharp division in the reconstituted Communist Party, with Rajk arguing for a radical anticoalition line.

Although the coalition policy had Stalin's full authority behind it, the issue during the early post-liberation period was by no means closed. While the Hungarian intra-Party debates were going on, Tito was demonstrating in Yugoslavia that a radical Communist leadership could nullify coalition agreements concluded under the auspices of the Big Three. During the war, Tito had been induced to sign an agreement with non-Communist members of King Peter's government-in-exile under which a Regency Council was set up and multi-party elections were to be held after the war. Stalin endorsed this agreement at Yalta. After Yugoslavia's liberation, the non-Communist leaders tried to reorganize their parties, but Tito's police prevented them from electioneering. In the end, they withdrew from the elections, and when the country went to the polls in November 1945, Tito's list of candidates was the only one on which people could vote. It would have been possible to achieve a similar result in Hungary had the same methods been employed, and it is safe to assume that the Hungarian comrades who "treated the coalition partners with antagonism"—that is, Rajk and his circle—had this kind of strategy in mind. Had they prevailed, the coalition stage would have been skipped in Hungary as it was in Yugoslavia, and the anticoalition stage might have been compressed into a few months instead of taking about two years. Since Rákosi was committed to slow, gradual procedure (he described it as "salami tactics" in his Academy speech of 1952), it would have been disastrous for him if Rajk had succeeded in forcing the pace. As things were, he managed to restrain the impatient underground, though apparently not without difficulty (the anticoalition attitude of the indigenous Communists, he said in his speech, had caused him "many difficulties"). For a few months, indeed, the Party's ranks had been split over the coalition issue, the home contingent remonstrating with the Muscovite group, even though afraid to challenge it openly. Was this the reason for Rákosi's later extermination campaign against the members of the wartime underground? In other words: did he do away with Rajk because Rajk was too radical?

24

From Coalition to Purge

Rajk as a Rival to Rákosi

The difference in outlook and temperament between the calculating bureaucrat Rákosi and the fanatical demagogue Rajk certainly brought a strain into their relationship. The original disagreement on the coalition issue, however, was a self-liquidating one. The non-Communist coalition partners were living on borrowed time; Rákosi himself was plotting their ruin even while he was assuring them of his amicable intentions. The "salami tactics" had their wonderful refinements of deceit and cruelty. "According to Béla Kovács [leader of the Smallholders Party] and his group," commented the Communist Party organ *Szabad Nép* on November 21, 1946, "the Communists are preparing to seize power. We have always said and still say that this is nonsense. The very fact that the democratic element in the Smallholders Party take this absurdity seriously shows how much they are under the influence of reactionary gossip."[13] In the following month, many leading Smallholders were arrested as fascist conspirators by Pálfy-Oesterreicher's military police, and in February 1947 Kovács himself was seized and abducted by the Russians. The anti-coalition campaign was on, and Rajk, as we have seen, played a leading part in it. At this stage the early disagreements about timing and tactics were no longer relevant.

If Rajk's group ever constituted a Left opposition within the Hungarian Communist Party, it certainly no longer did so in 1947 and 1948, when the liquidation of multi-party democracy was in full swing. But as the opposition issue was fading away, the rivalry issue was becoming more acute.

Important changes took place on the international scene in the spring of 1947. The Communists were ousted from the French and Italian governments in May; in June, the Marshall Plan was presented. The Soviet Union responded to these challenges by adopting a stiff anti-Western course. Moscow no longer thought it necessary to restrain the revolutionary ardor of Communist leaders such as Tito who had moved to establish the Communist single-party state too quickly. On the contrary, the changes in the West called for a Communist counteroffensive, to replace the multi-party regimes in the occupied countries and in Czechoslovakia by single-party ones as quickly as possible, and to integrate the whole area into a tightly controlled Soviet bloc. With the establishment of the Cominform in September 1947, the Communist counteroffensive was fully deployed.

Rákosi, of course, went along with the new, sharper policy, but his position was not secure. His rivals could exploit the new situation against him. Rajk could argue in Moscow that he rather than Rákosi was the logical leader in the changed circumstances; and others in high places who had been favoring a sharper course could rally to Rajk or combine with him. Until the break with Belgrade, the Soviet Union's Cominform policy amounted to an implicit endorsement of Tito's ultra-radicalism and an implicit condemnation of Rákosi's temporizing. This phase of the Cominform policy, therefore, posed a threat to Rákosi's position.

Rákosi managed to weather this crisis. From the spring of 1948 onward, when the break between Belgrade and Moscow was already impending, he was breathing more easily. He could now move to isolate Rajk, who, being identified with Tito's radical tendency, had become vulnerable.

The first logical step consisted in depriving Rajk of the police power which rendered him formidable. Against political enemies and coalition partners to be liquidated, Rajk's police was useful; but what would happen once there were no more outsiders to combat? Rákosi alerted the Hungarian Politburo to this danger. A report prepared by a Hungarian specialist describes the final stage of this action against Rajk in dramatic detail.

According to this report, the Politburo of the Hungarian

Communist Party was convened for a dawn meeting early in August 1948. Ernö Gerö, a prominent Muscovite but suspected of being Rákosi's rival, openly accused Rajk of preparing a *putsch* against the leadership. Rajk, Gerö said, had organized a special police force in the Radetzky barracks on Pálffy square. This force was receiving modern weapons, and was placed directly under Rajk rather than under the chief of police. Could there be any doubt about the use Rajk intended to make of it?

Rajk protested his loyalty: the special force existed, he admitted, but the Russians knew about it. This, of course, was not calculated to allay Rákosi's alarm. Finally, the issue was settled by Moscow. Rajk was to give up the Ministry of the Interior, but he was not to be purged; it was at Moscow's instance that he was made Foreign Minister.[14]

One of Rajk's close collaborators in the Foreign Ministry, whom I interviewed in 1957, gave a different account of Rajk's ouster from the Ministry of the Interior. Rajk, he said, was accused of a grave irregularity in organizing Communist policemen: instead of setting up special police cells reporting to the chief of the Party police apparatus, he ordered the policemen to enroll in whatever neighborhood cells operated at their places of residence. These neighborhood cells, of course, could not supervise what the policemen did while on the job; thus, Rajk's measure actually deprived the higher Party authorities of any effective control over police activities. Rajk, the informant said, admitted that his policy had been highly reprehensible from the Party's point of view, and was extremely contrite and upset about it. While in the Foreign Ministry, he seemed anxious above all to erase the bad impression his lapse had created and to redeem himself by acting as a perfectly loyal Party man.

This account must be considered authentic; there can be no doubt that the informant was relaying information he had from Rajk himself. Whether Rajk also organized a special police force, as the other report has it, cannot be determined; that his colleague did not refer to this in the interview does not prove that there was no such force. Rajk may have considered the matter too secret to mention even to a close collaborator. In any case, Rajk undoubtedly was building up a personal empire in the police, and the Old Guard around Rákosi, sensing the danger, took the control of the police out of his hands before he could use it as an instrument in the intra-Party struggle. To this extent, the rivalry hypothesis is certainly correct.

Was this rivalry a merely personal one, or did it also involve matters of principle? Even when the coalition issue was no longer of moment, another problem, that of national or state sovereignty, could well have separated indigenous Communists from Muscovites. Tito, in fact, not only disagreed with the Moscow center on the coalition issue; he was also a "national" Communist in the sense that he was determined to run Yugoslavia as a sovereign state, without Soviet agents planted in his political and administrative apparatus. It was on this issue that the conflict between Belgrade and Moscow came to a head. Were Rajk and the other salient figures in the indigenous Hungarian apparatus "Titoists" in this sense? They may indeed have had yearnings for "independence"; but Budapest was not Belgrade. The issue of running Hungary without Soviet interference could not arise so long as the Soviet authorities were firmly entrenched everywhere. And, according to Rajk's collaborator in the Foreign Ministry, Rajk was scrupulously loyal to the Soviets.

Purging the Powerless

In any case, Rajk was no longer a dangerous rival by the summer of 1949, the time of his arrest and framing as an accomplice of Tito and a fascist police spy of long standing. He no longer had police power, and his main concern appears to have been to regain the leadership's confidence. For the last

28

stage, then, the loyalty hypothesis seems to hold insofar as Rajk himself is concerned, and no other assumption is possible as regards Rajk's former civilian associates in the home underground whose turn to be purged came in 1951.* When Rákosi moved to eliminate this group, it represented no coherent ideological front in the Party and commanded no power position. Of course, this is not to say that Rajk had *never* been a danger to Rákosi, or that he or his circle could not have become a danger again if circumstances changed. It is probable, indeed, that Rákosi thought it safest to eliminate all those elements in the Party that had a distinct physiognomy of their own and a past different from his; for, as long as such elements existed, Moscow's eye could always fall on them as a possible alternative to him and his circle. Rákosi's position was particularly vulnerable because of his Jewish origin; in fact, all the top leaders of the Hungarian Communist Party—Gerö, Révai, and Farkas, in whose hands, next to Rákosi himself, all real political power was concentrated—were Jews. Although the Soviet regime officially repudiated anti-Semitism, there had been a strong anti-Jewish undercurrent in Soviet politics since Stalin consolidated his power. Zhdanov's campaign against "rootless cosmopolitans," a transparent code name for Jews, gave this trend public prominence, and it boded no good for Rákosi that the Cominform bloc had been launched under Zhdanov's auspices. The break with Tito, however, enabled Rákosi to reconsolidate his position by discovering a vast "Titoist" conspiracy within the Hungarian Party, a conspiracy headed by his potential rival, Rajk.

It is a rule of the totalitarian game of politics that no issue is joined before the outcome appears absolutely certain. Be-

* Things were different insofar as the former *military* underground was concerned: Pálfy-Oesterreicher, who was tried and executed shortly after Rajk, had built up a special police force and thus was decidedly a "rival."

fore proceeding to a purge, totalitarian politicians always make certain that their rivals and prospective victims are isolated and deprived of the possibility of effective defense. As a rule, neither ideological and policy differences nor power rivalries are publicly aired in totalitarian parties as long as they are live issues; such divisions manifest themselves in backstage maneuverings, while the façade of monolithic unity is carefully maintained. The existence of a rift is acknowledged only when the losers of backstage maneuvers are stripped of power. At that point, the winning group does all it can to make the division appear as grave and fateful as possible: the intra-party opposition, once destroyed, is presented to the party rank-and-file and to the world at large as a brood of criminals of the darkest hue, in league with the forces of evil.

The Rajk purge conformed to this classic pattern. It involved a sudden shift from the public image of complete harmony to the satanic myth of a monster unmasked. It is irrelevant whether there may have been a small factual nucleus for the myth. The real political issues that existed at one time or another between the Rajk group and the top leadership could have been settled without resort to demonology. The significance of the purge and its official justification applied to the future rather than the past. The purge and the official myth created around it served to strengthen Rákosi's position, to prove to the rank-and-file that he was the undisputed master, while convincing Moscow that no acceptable leadership material existed in the Hungarian Communist Party outside his group.

This strategy, and the brutal surgery that it led to within the Hungarian Party, caused a grave psychological crisis in the rank-and-file. Friends of the victims, as some of them stated in interviews with me, could not imagine that these men were guilty; yet they had to force themselves to believe the charges in order to preserve their Communist faith. As to the victims themselves, the treatment meted out to them turned them into fierce enemies of the leadership, even though most of them had been loyal enough to begin with. Rákosi, however, was not concerned with the feelings of Party members sitting behind bars; how could these people ever turn the tables on him? Nor was it conceivable to him that the victims' friends would ever dare to reopen the issue. In Stalin's lifetime, such repercussions were wholly unimaginable. If the purge created any adverse feelings, there seemed to be no possibility that these would ever come out into the open. The only conceivable aftermath was fear and silence, a good enough basis for Party unity under the leader's undisputed authority.

The Return of the Victims

Developments after Stalin's death revealed the flaw in these calculations. The advent of "collective leadership" in the Soviet Union led to the liberation of large numbers of victims of intra-Party purges throughout the Soviet bloc and to the devaluation or even complete repudiation of the purge myths. Those responsible for the purges suddenly found themselves under attack; Stalin's death had ushered in the period of the "anti-purge purges."[15]

In Hungary, the leadership of the secret police (the AVH) was thoroughly shaken up: in March 1954, Gábor Péter, the head of the AVH, was removed and sentenced to life imprisonment, and about fifty high police officers were jailed. On the other hand, Party members and sympathizers imprisoned on trumped-up charges during the purge wave of 1949–51 were released. As we shall see, the return of the purge victims from concentration camps, and their readmission into the Party, created an explosive atmosphere that corroded Rákosi's authority. The division in the Party's ranks caused by the reappearance of the purge victims was an essential part of the "elite pattern" of the revolution.

THE RIGHT OPPOSITION

The Party Career of an Oppositionist

The division between the indigenous underground and the Muscovite group around Rákosi was not the only one that existed within the Hungarian Communist Party during the 1945–49 period. In standard Communist parlance, the Rajk circle represented a "left" opposition, and this group was most vocal when the Party's policy was, temporarily, steering a "right" (coalition) course. However, as the official policy became more and more "leftist" and radical, a "right" opposition trend also appeared. This Right opposition warned against forcing the tempo of the "socialist" transformation of Hungary. It argued against overambitious industrialization policies and, above all, against the forcible collectivization of agriculture.

The leading figure of the Right opposition was Imre Nagy, the future Prime Minister and tragic hero of the 1956 revolution. He was himself a member of the Muscovite group, and as such entered Hungarian politics at the top level: he became a member of the Politburo of the reconstituted Party and was one of the few Communists in the first coalition cabinets of the post-liberation era. Between 1947 and 1951, his career was in eclipse; he was dropped from the cabinet and for a while also from the Politburo and the Central Committee. In the great purges, however, he was spared. Though he held no political post, he was permitted to lecture on economics at an agrarian university near Budapest. Strangely enough, Nagy emerged from political exile in 1950–51, when Rákosi was supreme and his terror reached its climax.

How can this odd sequence of events be explained? There can be no doubt that Nagy was eliminated from the ruling group because he persistently opposed Rákosi's radical policy line. After presenting the available evidence for this, I shall try to answer the question why Nagy was not purged and why he was eventually readmitted to favor.

From Coalition to Purge

Imre Nagy and the NEP

As regards the policy disagreements between Nagy and Rákosi, we have Nagy's own account in a lengthy memorandum he composed in 1955–56 after some further spectacular ups and downs in his career: Prime Minister from July 1953 to April 1955, he was expelled from the Party in November 1955, and the memorandum in question was written as a brief arguing for his readmission.[16]

Nagy's analysis of the conflict between him and Rákosi starts from the premise that ever since the liberation Hungary had been in a "transitional period," for which the principles of Lenin's New Economic Policy (NEP), rather than those of later Soviet policies, were valid.

> Thus the NEP is the specific means and form of building socialism, and is absolutely necessary in every country where there is a significantly large number of small peasants. Consequently, during the transitional period, the NEP is the basis for our entire economic policy. This means that the elements of the NEP are not operative to the same extent throughout the entire transitional period, but wither away to the extent that the building of socialism proceeds and to the extent that the socialist sectors of the economy develop.[17]

Nagy criticizes Rákosi's economic policies—the ambitious Five-Year Plan of 1950, revised upward in 1951, and the accelerated collectivization of agriculture—as running counter to "Lenin's teachings." According to these, "the NEP represents a certain compromise, but a compromise without which socialism cannot be victorious."[18] Socialism cannot win unless a satisfactory relationship is built up between the industrial sector and the peasantry; this, however, requires the maintenance of a market economy "because, as Lenin frequently said, the small commodity producers will tolerate no economic ties to socialist industry except ties through merchandise, which normally result in trade."[19]

33

Party Debates on the NEP

In his book, Nagy presents his criticism of Rákosi's policies in general and retrospective terms. He does not refer to any internal Party debates that took place when the shift to a radical course was under deliberation, nor does he mention the fact that in these debates he himself took a strong stand against the shift. A Communist source, however, gives some interesting details about this early clash between Nagy and Rákosi and about Nagy's resulting demotion. The matter is discussed by Dezsö Nemes, candidate member of the Politburo of the Hungarian Communist Party, in an article that was published in a Soviet historical journal a few months after the announcement of Nagy's execution in June 1958.[20]

Nemes summarizes Nagy's position as follows:

> When in 1947–48 the country entered on the road of socialist construction, Imre Nagy took a stand in the Central Committee against this course, although Hungary's whole historical development indicated it to be the only proper one. Imre Nagy put forward the thesis that the construction of socialism in Hungary was not a problem for the time, that historically it was not yet on the agenda. According to him, the country at that time was facing merely a bourgeois-democratic transformation; the nationalization of industry in People's Hungary represented allegedly not a socialist but a state-capitalist development. From this false thesis he drew the conclusion that there was no contradiction between socialized industrial production and private agriculture; consequently, that to put the socialist transformation of agriculture on the agenda was untimely.[21]

The argument here attributed to Nagy amounts to a cynical rejection of all socialist principles; its gist is: "Our so-called socialized industry is capitalist in its essence, so why not leave agriculture capitalistic too?" It is inconceivable that anybody could have argued along such lines in a Communist policy-making body. Nemes's purpose was to put words in Nagy's mouth that would convict him as a counterrevolutionary before a Soviet audience; his version of the policy line advocated by Nagy was calculated to be as shocking as possible. This procedure is prescribed by the peculiar logic of Soviet-Communist Party history. Actually, everybody in internal Party debates argues along Marxist-Leninist lines, but the Party historian must not reproduce the Marxist-Leninist arguments used by people subsequently condemned as wreckers and internal enemies. To do so would be tantamount to admitting the possibility of a genuinely Marxist-Leninist opposition within the Party; and this is precisely what no Soviet-Communist Party historian must ever admit. He must strip the position of the so-called wreckers of any Marxist underpinnings and present it as the out-and-out pro-capitalist one that it "objectively" (to use Party language) is.

If we try to reconstruct Nagy's position from his own book, it appears most likely that in 1947–48 he was trying to stop Rákosi's extreme plans, notably as regards the collectivization of agriculture, on the grounds that anything going beyond Lenin's NEP policy was impracticable under the conditions then prevailing in Hungary. In other words, he probably was pleading for the maintenance of a private market for agricultural products (as well as for a private sector for trade in consumer goods in general) at the same time that he favored the nationalization of large industries and financial institutions. Such a program obviously went far beyond a mere "bourgeois revolution," although it did fall short of integral socialization.

It seems that the debate on NEP *vs.* integral socialization was over by September 1949. Nemes reports that the Central Committee met at that time and called Nagy on the carpet for advocating "anti-Marxist views." We recall that the Rajk wing was liquidated about the same time: after getting rid of his rival on the "left," Rákosi moved to silence his critic on the "right" as well. According to Nemes, Nagy defended himself against the charge of having denied the "socialist" character of nationalized industries, but still held out against the persecution of the middle peasants.

Imre Nagy in essence defended the free development of the middle peasant economy into a kulak one, and on this opportunist basis wanted to "strengthen" the alliance [of the working class] with the middle peasant. Therefore he characterized the capitalist tendencies [of the peasantry] as insignificant and allegedly bound to disappear automatically in the small and middle peasant economy; therefore also he came out against exaggerating the kulak danger.[22]

"Relying on Leninist principles," the Central Committee plenum, firmly controlled by Rákosi, "rightly rejected the rotten views on the policy and attitudes of the middle peasant put forward by Imre Nagy." His position having been formally condemned, Nagy admitted his error. The Central Committee, accepting his self-criticism as sincere, removed him from the Politburo and the Central Committee "for a short while" only.[23] Actually, Nagy was back in the cabinet as Minister of Collective Production (in charge of forced agricultural deliveries) in 1950;[24] his restoration to his Party offices took place the following year.

Nemes makes much of Nagy's collaboration with Rákosi following their clash in 1948–49; he tries to lay at Nagy's door part of the responsibility for some of the most outrageous of Rákosi's policies, such as the adoption of a ruinous Five-Year Plan in 1950 and its upward revision in 1951. Nagy's assumption of the office of Minister of Collective Production is presented as proof that by 1951 Nagy had become a Rákosist, only to revert back to his pro-kulak position in June 1953.

A Tentative Explanation of Nagy's Demotion and Recall

All this is not easy to understand. To begin with: why did the Central Committee let Nagy off so lightly after seeing through his "rotten," "anti-Leninist" opportunism? Nemes himself raises this question:

> A principled struggle directed against the wavering of the small bourgeoisie and aimed at attracting it to the side of the people's power required public criticism of the roots of the rotten anti-Leninist views of Imre Nagy. However, such a criticism did not follow. The question arises why the Central Committee did not reveal thoroughly the opportunist essence of the political conceptions of Imre Nagy.[25]

Nemes suggests that the Central Committee, "while rejecting the opportunist views of Imre Nagy," failed at the same time to "examine in the necessary way the question of the alliance with private working peasants under the conditions existing in Hungary in the period of development of the productive cooperative [kolkhoz] movement." But this does not answer the question; the fact that the Central Committee, won over to the policy of all-out collectivization, failed to think about an "alliance" with the working private peasants in no way explains why Nagy was not purged. On the contrary: being oblivious to the necessity of an "alliance" with the peasantry, the Central Committee might be expected to be maximally harsh with Nagy.

Nagy's alleged changeover to an extreme antipeasant policy, followed by a reversion to his original stand, also is a mystery. The record (including Nemes's own account) shows that Nagy was stubbornly consistent in upholding his conception of a Hungarian NEP. He clung to this position against the strongest pressure, both in the intra-Party debates of 1947–49 and during all the later stages of his tragic career; he did not recant even to save his life. His brief period of collaboration with Rákosi (1950–53) cannot be explained in terms of an "opportunistic" change of orientation.

What, then, is the real explanation of Nagy's temporary demotion in 1949 and his subsequent reinstatement in 1951?

The following assumptions would seem to fit the facts most closely.

In 1949, Moscow fully approved of Rákosi's sharp policy of forced industrialization and collectivization. This was required by the logic of the Soviet government's over-all political strategy at that time; being squeezed out of the power positions it had held during the early postwar period in Western Europe, including West Germany, the Communist center responded by setting up a satellite empire fully integrated in an Eastern bloc. Rákosi obtained Stalin's favor by the extraordinary zeal he showed in Sovietizing Hungary. Yet the Moscow center apparently was reluctant to allow him to liquidate his rivals and opponents on the Right as well as the Left. Perhaps Stalin considered it advisable to keep an alternative to Rákosi available in the Hungarian Party. At any rate, the Party's failure to make a public issue of Nagy's opposition can be explained only by assuming that he had powerful protection in Moscow.

Since Nagy could not be liquidated, it was best for Rákosi not to keep him out of active politics for any length of time. After the loss of his Party offices, Nagy was appointed professor of agrarian economics at an agricultural academy, where he was in a position to influence students. Moreover, he was the only top-ranking Communist who did not live apart from the people but kept up relations with a wide circle of acquaintances in ordinary walks of life; he also was a familiar figure in the Budapest cafés. It was dangerous to have such a maverick around, and putting him in charge of forced agricultural deliveries appeared the surest way to blight his growing popularity with the peasantry.

Nagy was probably not in a position to reject Rákosi's advances; had he done so, he would have provoked a final break, and Moscow in all probability would not have protected him. Possibly, like so many people who collaborate with regimes they know to be evil, he persuaded himself that he could at least "prevent the worst" by taking the office offered to him. At any rate, Nagy behaved in thoroughly conformist fashion after his comeback. At a Party meeting in the Budapest Opera House, he denounced Western "aggression" in Korea, eulogized the Soviet Union, and prophesied the early collapse of capitalism. On the morning after Stalin's death, it was he who delivered the eulogy before the Hungarian parliament, referring to Stalin as the "great leader of all humanity."[26] Nagy's return to the fold was the crowning triumph for Rákosi, who, it seemed, no longer had to contend with any challengers in the Party.

3

THE NEW COURSE

AND ITS

AFTERMATH

As long as Stalin was alive, the intra-elite conflicts in Hungary could not affect the stability of the regime. Rákosi was able to neutralize both the Left and the Right opposition: Rajk was liquidated and Nagy was forced to submit. There were no unresolved issues, either of policy or of personal rivalry. After Stalin's death, however, the situation changed. Stalin's successors made drastic changes in the government of Hungary: they substituted dual leadership for Rákosi's centralized, one-man rule. By doing this, they unwittingly undermined the stability of the Hungarian Communist regime; for dual leadership reopened the old issues that were seemingly settled forever, without permitting them to be settled on a new basis.

RÁKOSI'S POLICY CONDEMNED

There had been dissatisfaction in Moscow with Rákosi's conduct of Hungarian affairs for some time before Stalin's death. The country's economic situation was extremely bad. Rákosi's overambitious industrialization projects were bleeding the country white. A new steel center was erected at Dunapentele, a small river town south of Budapest, appropriately renamed Sztalinváros; other huge projects (power plants, chemical combines) were started elsewhere. Hungary lacked all the basic raw materials (iron ore, coking coal, and so on) to put this new industrial capacity to use; the construction itself cost enormous sums and absorbed far more manpower than the country could spare. True, some industrialization was needed to siphon off the surplus agrarian population, but in Hungary the rate was excessive. The number of people employed in industry rose from 808,000 in 1950 to 1,124,000 in 1955;[1] the shifting of more than 300,000 agricultural producers to urban industries crippled agriculture. The situation was aggravated by the fact that the peasants remaining on the land, exasperated and harassed by forced collectivization, reduced their output. The new industries did not help to restore the balance, since they either could not start production at all or, at any rate, could not produce goods for export that could have been exchanged for foodstuffs. Thus, the general standard of living declined disastrously. Prices went up in relation to money wages. In the cities, there were chronic shortages, and in the countryside, which had been swept bare by forced deliveries, conditions were such that the peasants themselves were nearly starving. Reports about the Hungarian situation supplied by the Soviet Embassy in Budapest fully apprised the Moscow leadership of the gravity of the crisis, and the Moscow center became more and more impatient with Rákosi.

MOSCOW INTERVENES

In the spring of 1953, things were ripe for a change: something had to be done to avert complete collapse. It was the new government in Moscow, dominated by Malenkov and Beria, that told the Hungarians what to do. Rákosi was called to Moscow in June *ad audiendum verbum*. The reorganization of the government was the main item on the agenda: Hungary, like the rest of the Communist bloc, was to adopt collective

41

leadership. This meant that Rákosi could not hope to retain both the premiership and the office of Party leader. Moscow, moreover, was not in a mood to accept a candidate for the premiership proposed by Rákosi and subservient to him. He was told to bring along with him to Moscow his old critic Imre Nagy (back in the Politburo since 1951), two Politburo members of the Stalinist Old Guard (Ernö Gerö and Mihály Farkas), and the Chairman of the Presidium, István Dobi, formerly a member of the Smallholders Party.

Appearing before the Presidium with his ill-matched companions, Rákosi was forced to listen to a scathing denunciation of his stewardship during the past years. Beria, Malenkov, Molotov, Khrushchev, and Kaganovich took him severely to task. He was told that his attempt to build up a gigantic heavy industry in Hungary was unsound, extravagant adventurism. Forced collectivization had brought about a decline in agriculture. If the situation was not remedied, Khrushchev said, the government would eventually be "booted out."[2]

The Hungarian delegation returned to Budapest with precise instructions: the Central Committee was to meet and condemn Rákosi's policy of overindustrialization and forced collectivization as well as the excesses of the secret police. Rákosi was to give up the premiership; Farkas and Gerö, the two powerful Old Guard figures who had accompanied him, also were instructed to relinquish their cabinet posts (the ministries of Defense and Heavy Industry, respectively). The Minister of Culture, József Révai, who was not in Moscow, was to be retired from the Politburo and the government. Rákosi, Farkas, and Gerö, however, were confirmed in their Party offices; thus Rákosi remained First Secretary of the Party, and the others kept their seats in the Politburo and the Central Committee. The premiership was bestowed upon Nagy.

It was more than displeasure with Rákosi's policies that prompted Moscow to order a cabinet shake-up. The fact that

Mátyás Rákosi was of Jewish origin and that he had filled all the top positions with Jews also had been a black mark against him in Moscow. The Presidium members reportedly taunted him with his Jewish origin at the Moscow meeting, Beria remarking: "We know that there have been in Hungary, apart from its own rulers, Turkish sultans, Austrian emperors, Tartar khans, and Polish princes. But, as far as we know, Hungary has never had a Jewish king. Apparently, this is what you have become. Well, you can be sure that we won't allow it."[3] It apparently weighed much in Nagy's favor that he was of Hungarian peasant stock.

Nagy's primary task was to placate the peasantry by stopping the collectivization drive. By giving him this mission, the Moscow center completely vindicated his earlier stand, for which he had been censured in 1948–49. In all other respects, too, the governmental program drawn up in Moscow followed the "NEP" principle that Nagy had advocated before. In economic policy, there would be greater emphasis upon consumer goods; respect for personal rights would be restored, and the victims of police terror would be freed. The government, headed by Nagy, and the Party apparatus under Rákosi were instructed to collaborate in carrying out the new program.

The Moscow decisions were promptly put into effect by the Central Committee of the Hungarian Communist Party. The required resolution was passed on June 28; on July 4, Nagy was appointed Premier and announced the new policy before the parliament. Rákosi's position seemed to have been compromised beyond repair. He did, however, manage to ward off the worst: it was decided, at his insistence, that the text of the June resolution would not be published. In his address to the parliament, Nagy gave only a toned-down version of it. Rákosi's disgrace was thus mitigated; the door was not closed to his eventual return to greater influence. For the time being, however, his stewardship did stand condemned.

The New Course and Its Aftermath

Nagy's inaugural speech amounted to a scathing denunciation of the Rákosi government's policies. Basic changes were needed in every field, he declared; to begin with, forced industrialization had to be abandoned:

> We have to realize and admit openly before the country that the objectives of the increased Five-Year Plan in many respects go beyond our forces, that to pursue them puts an undue strain upon our resources and not only hinders the development of material welfare but in recent times has brought about a decline in the standard of living. It is evident that there must be a fundamental change in this respect. The building-up of socialized heavy industry cannot be an end in itself. . . . Excessive industrialization and the striving for industrial autarky are in no way justified, especially since we lack the necessary raw materials. . . . We must considerably slow down the development of industries manufacturing producers' goods and put much greater emphasis upon light industries and food industries producing consumer goods, so as to be increasingly able to satisfy the growing needs of the population.[4]

Nagy then turned to the explosive issue of agricultural policy. He assailed Rákosi's collectivization program, for which "both economic and political foundations were lacking." Although agricultural production was still based mainly upon individual farming, the government not only did nothing to help the individual farmer, but persecuted him. The authorities committed excesses and resorted to violent pressures which "outraged the peasantry's sense of justice." Determined to change this, the new government prohibited the usual "fall reapportionment campaign,"* and decided to slow down the tempo of collectivization:

---

* Obligatory reapportionment was one of the methods applied by the Rákosi regime in its efforts to uproot the individual peasants. Under this system, the government periodically expropriated parts of peasant holdings and gave their owners distant and inferior tracts of land in return, the best land being turned over to state farms.

44

In the interests of strict observance of the principle of voluntary collectivization, the government will make it possible for kolkhoz members to withdraw from the kolkhozes after the harvest if that is their wish. In addition to this, the government will also permit the dissolution of kolkhozes when the majority of the members desire it.

Another concession to the peasantry announced by Nagy was the abolition of the "kulak lists." Inclusion in such a list was ruinous for the private farmer because it subjected him to crippling disabilities (exclusion from credit, from the distribution of fertilizer, and so on) as well as to constant harassment.

For other groups and the population at large, too, the "New Course" announced by Nagy brought significant alleviations. In order to improve the supply of goods and services in the cities, the government issued licenses for small handicraft and retail establishments. Intellectuals and professional people were to be treated with greater consideration. Above all, Nagy promised to do away with violations of "legality" perpetrated by the police organs of the regime, and with the "excesses, abuses, and other acts of harassment that hurt the population's sense of justice and opened up a gap between the toiling people and the state organs and local councils." The new program contemplated the revision of cases of unjustly imprisoned people, the abolition of internment camps, and the liberation of political prisoners whose offenses were not serious.

Nagy's speech caused an enormous sensation. Understandably enough, the New Course was extremely popular in the cities, since it promised tangible, immediate improvements. The peasantry, however, instead of passively waiting for the promised governmental measures whereby the reform would be put into practice, read Nagy's speech as the regime's admission of weakness and defeat, and went over to the offensive. Many peasants in the villages concluded that "Communism was over" and proceeded to divide the collectivized land, equipment, and livestock among themselves.[5] The peasants took advantage of the fact that harvesting had just begun; they tried to force the hand of the authorities by refusing to bring in the harvest unless and until their goal of decollectivization was attained. The government was thoroughly alarmed. It reminded the peasants that the dissolution of kolkhozes was to be authorized only after the harvest season, and then only within the framework of certain rules and regulations; independent action was prohibited. There were numerous clashes in the countryside during the week following Nagy's speech.

At first, the regime's newspapers kept silent about the disorders; there was only an insistent press campaign about the necessity of speeding up the grain harvest: any delay would result in grave losses of precious grain. The lagging of the harvest was attributed to widespread misconceptions about the right moment for cutting the grain.[6] The communist newspapers reassured their readers that the kolkhoz peasants had no desire to decollectivize the land, even after the government had announced that they were free to do so. It was only after several days that references to rioting began to appear in the press. In an editorial of July 13, the Party organ, *Szabad Nép*, admitted that "the enemy is trying with all his might to disturb the execution of our program." A report published on July 18 finally spoke about "kulaks" and "backward elements" among kolkhoz peasants who resisted the authorities, and mentioned kolkhozes on which members of harvesting brigades had gone on strike.

RÁKOSI VERSUS NAGY

After the stormy sequel to the launching of the New Course by Nagy, Rákosi took advantage of the situation to rally the Party apparatus against the forces of reform. He defined his position at a meeting of the *Aktiv* of the Budapest Party organization on July 11, 1953. His task was by no means easy. Moscow's decisions, and the Central Committee's resolutions of June 27–28, were still in force, and Rákosi was under an obligation to engage in self-criticism. Yet, even as he did so, he managed to convey the thesis that Nagy's program merely reflected the *government's* interpretation of the resolutions, and that only he, Rákosi himself, spoke with the Party's authentic voice. He completely agreed with Nagy's criticism, to be sure, and it was undeniable that the Party had committed mistakes. Yet the main thing was that the Party should now close ranks against those elements which would take advantage of the New Course to demolish socialism itself.

On the kolkhoz issue, in particular, Rákosi covertly challenged Nagy, while overtly emphasizing his complete agreement with him. Nagy in his speech had treated the collective farms as expendable; Rákosi treated them as the cornerstone of "village socialism." He admitted that a number of peasants had only joined the kolkhozes under duress (which was deplorable), but then went on to say:

> We address ourselves in particular to the Communists within the agricultural cooperatives, their party organization, the Communist Youth League members and their organizations, and the tractor drivers and combine operators, calling upon them to take a strong stand in the struggle for the defense and strengthening of the cooperatives. They should always be in the front ranks, and unmask and repel in a courageous and energetic fashion every manifestation and attack of the enemy. They must not yield to discouragement, nor succumb to the hostile propaganda that is now being issued in an effort to exploit the good work we have done and launch an attack upon the entire cooperative movement. . . .
>
> We shall not stand by idly while the enemy is trying to undermine the results thus far achieved in the construction of village socialism. We shall not tolerate any anticooperative agitation, just as we do not tolerate any agitation against the construction of socialism. . . .

47

The fact that we have proposed the abolition of the kulak lists has made these exploiters of the village think that their release has come. We must see to it that they are speedily disabused of these false notions.[7]

The implications of Rákosi's speech were not lost on the Party apparatus: the New Course as represented by the Nagy government was not that of the Party corps. Thus, instead of collective leadership, there was now an open split within the Party. Rákosi kept his cohorts together and told them that Nagy was a dangerous schismatic against whom the Party functionaries had to defend socialism. At the same time, the ministerial bureaucracy and the Communist intelligentsia in general supported Nagy. Thus throughout Nagy's premiership a state of latent crisis prevailed. He was unable to get rid of Rákosi or even to discipline him. Nagy did not control the Party's disciplinary apparatus; to use terroristic police methods against Rákosi was wholly out of the question, since keeping the police out of intra-Party struggles was one of the key points of Moscow's new policy. Rákosi, on the other hand, could well hope to resolve the crisis by undermining Nagy in Moscow.

In fact, soon after launching his anti-Nagy campaign in the Party in July 1953, Rákosi felt he had good reason to assume that the situation in Moscow had already changed decisively in his favor: Beria, who had been his main accuser at the Presidium meeting, was liquidated. As it turned out, however, Moscow's Hungarian policy remained unchanged even after Beria's fall. In the spring of 1954, the Hungarian Communist Party called a Party congress at which a new Politburo was to be elected; at Moscow's wish, three of Rákosi's henchmen were to be dropped. Rákosi obtained a postponement of the congress and went to Moscow in May to plead his case: he had been blackened by Beria, who had since been proved a traitor; the center ought to revise its verdict. This time it was Khrushchev who answered Rákosi. He told him in effect that

Beria, though undoubtedly a traitor, had been quite right insofar as he, Rákosi, was concerned.[8] After this, the Hungarian Party Congress dropped the three Rákosite Politburo members, and the policy of rehabilitating the Communist victims of Rákosi's purges continued in force.

RÁKOSI'S COMEBACK: THE CRISIS PERSISTS

Nagy was clearly still in Moscow's favor in the autumn of 1954, since the Central Committee, whose decisions always reflected Moscow's views, upheld him at its October meeting. Rákosi, apparently decisively beaten, left for Soviet Russia, ostensibly for reasons of health. While in Russia, however, he perceived an opportunity for resuming his efforts to unseat Nagy. Khrushchev, Bulganin, and Mikoyan, who had visited Peiping in October, were understood in Party circles to have reached an agreement among themselves, and possibly also with Mao, to eliminate Malenkov and revert to the pre-Malenkov economic policy of assigning top priority to the expansion of heavy industry. Rákosi felt sure that if this line were adopted, Nagy would be finished in Hungary, and he, Rákosi, would again enjoy Moscow's favor. He now sought out Kaganovich (one of Malenkov's chief opponents) and supplied him with information about the very difficult economic situation (inflationary pressures, currency shortage, and so on) that had been created in Hungary by Nagy's liberalizing course.[9] This information could be useful in undermining Malenkov; if Malenkov were overthrown, Nagy's fall, too, would be inevitable.

Rákosi's intrigues were fully successful. As the cabal against Malenkov gained ground, the Hungarian leaders were summoned to Moscow once more to receive instructions on how to change their policy and reorganize their government. The Hungarian group that appeared before the Presidium on January 7, 1955, was almost identical in its composition with the one that had gone to Moscow in June 1953; its members were Nagy, Rákosi, Gerö, Farkas, and a younger member of the Party secretariat, Béla Szalai, who had also accompanied the earlier group.[10] On the Soviet side, too, the same people were present in 1955 as in 1953, except for Beria's absence and Bulganin's presence. The burden of the Russians' message, however, was the exact reverse of what it had been in 1953. This time, Moscow assailed Nagy for having ruined the country's economy and damaged the Party's morale by his excessive liberalization. Characteristically, the chief critic was Malenkov, who was himself closely associated with a policy line very much like the one he was now attacking. Obviously under strong pressure from his colleagues, Malenkov castigated Nagy for a number of ideological mistakes. The Presidium then instructed the Hungarians to correct their policies at once; that is, to stop the costly conversion of industries to consumer goods production and, instead, use the available plant for what it had been chiefly designed for, namely, military production. There was, however, no question of replacing Nagy. Because of his Jewish origin, among other reasons, Rákosi could not be made Premier again, and no third candidate of sufficient stature was available.

Nevertheless, Moscow's censure had begun to undermine Nagy's position, and Malenkov's subsequent fall was to weaken it still further. Later in January of 1955, Nagy suffered a heart attack, and his illness gave Rákosi an opportunity for feverishly mobilizing opposition against him in the Central Committee. In view of the rebuke that Moscow had administered to Nagy, this was not very difficult. Meeting on March 2–4, the Central Committee censored Nagy as a "right deviationist" who had supported "anti-Marxist conceptions."[11]

Although Nagy nominally remained in office as Premier after the censure, in point of fact, being ill, he was unable to attend to any business, and his colleagues kept him in ignorance about what was going on.[12] As to why he was not ousted from office at once, the only plausible explanation seems to be that the Russians did not desire a change. Voroshilov, according to an informant, visited Budapest on April 4 to attend Liberation Day celebrations; noticing that Nagy's picture was not among those displayed in the streets, he expressed his disapproval, with the result that hundreds of pictures of Nagy were rounded up and exhibited. After Voroshilov's departure, this informant said, Rákosi obtained Nagy's dismissal from the Central Committee and the Hungarian parliament simply by asserting that he had Voroshilov's oral authorization for this move. At any rate, the Central Committee dismissed Nagy from all Party offices, and, on April 18, parliament relieved him of his post as Premier and appointed an unknown younger man, András Hegedüs, to succeed him. Hegedüs, an agricultural economist, had come out of the indigenous Party. His principal qualification for the premiership seems to have been that he was not a Jew. With Hegedüs at the head of the cabinet, Rákosi was again top man, for Hegedüs was not the one to pursue an independent line. According to an informant, he spent most of his time in his office studying the Moscow newspapers.

Rákosi's comeback, however, did not mean that he regained the full measure of his former power. The split during the New Course period had left enduring marks, and the ministerial bureaucracy remained committed to the liberalizing tendency of Nagy. Moreover, Soviet policy was evolving in a direction potentially dangerous for Rákosi. As we have seen, Rákosi had sought to retain Moscow's favor in 1949 by exterminating alleged Titoists and blackening Tito's name; in 1955, however, the Kremlin was cultivating Tito's friendship, and Rákosi's anti-Titoist record became a liability for him. Tito, who hated him, now had enough influence in Moscow to make sure that Rákosi would not again be allowed to resort to purges or to proceed forcefully against his opponents; and his opponents now were both many and outspoken.

The New Course and Its Aftermath

There were, to begin with, the rehabilitated Communist victims of the great purges who had been released from prisons and internment camps in batches during the New Course period. Moscow had decided that these people were to be readmitted to the Party and could even be appointed to political and Party offices. In this way, János Kádár, who had helped to frame his friend Rajk but subsequently had been purged himself, became secretary of one of the Budapest Party branches. Others in the same category were the former underground members Géza Losonczy, Sándor Haraszti, Ferenc Donáth, and Szilárd Ujhelyi, all of whom rose to some political prominence under Nagy. (Losonczy, for example, became head of the "Patriotic People's Front," created, or rather revived, in August 1954 to serve as a mass organization in which non-Party people could engage in some kind of political activity under Communist supervision.) These former purge victims were understandably indignant over Rákosi's maneuvers that had brought down their rescuer Nagy, and they now had some influence within the Party. In fact, the gruesome details of their ordeal, which gradually became known throughout the Party, horrified many insiders, creating more and more new enemies for Rákosi.

There were also stirrings among the lower functionaries of the Party, particularly in Budapest and the other industrial centers. Of working-class origin themselves, and living in close contact with the workers, the lower Party functionaries knew how the people felt about the abandonment of the New Course.

Finally, a new and formidable enemy of the top leadership appeared on the periphery of the apparatus: the Communist intellectuals who had deeply sympathized with the New Course and were not reconciled to its liquidation in the spring of 1955. They challenged the leadership on this issue with increasing boldness, and the ferment stirred up by them contributed much to the disintegration of the leadership's authority in the summer of 1956.

The New Course and Its Aftermath

The intellectuals had only an insignificant power base within the Party: they were supposed to implement the directives handed down from above, not to make policy. Still, it was the Party members enrolled in the Writers' Association, a supposedly nonpolitical, professional body, who ran that organization and controlled its mouthpiece, the weekly *Irodalmi Ujság* (Literary Gazette). The Party organization within the Writers' Association also directed the editorial policy of the other literary, artistic, and cultural magazines in Hungary, such as *Béke és Szabadság* (Peace and Freedom), *Szinház és Mozi* (Theater and Cinema), *Uj Hang* (New Voice), *Müvelt Nép* (Cultured People), and *Csillag* (Star). All these organs eventually participated in the intellectuals' campaign against Rákosi and the top leadership.

The other organizational base available to the dissenting Communist intellectuals was the Communist Youth League (DISZ), or rather a committee of this organization, the Petöfi Circle Committee, which maintained a discussion club in Budapest called the Petöfi Circle. In the spring of 1956, shortly after the Twentieth Party Congress in the Soviet Union, the Committee, seventeen of whose twenty members were Party members,[13] transformed the Circle into a public forum, where the regime was relentlessly denounced.

It was an unprecedented phenomenon in the history of Communist regimes to have a subordinate Party organ, such as the Party organization in a professional body, emancipate itself from the top leadership's control and defy it in public. That this was possible showed how incomplete Rákosi's comeback really was: he could not dismiss the intellectual rebels out of hand. The Party's repressive apparatus was still immensely strong and would have crushed any opposition movement from the non-Communist mass without difficulty. But in 1955–56, as we shall see, it was not possible to use that repressive apparatus against insiders. Hence, organized opposition operating from power bases within the Party was possible, and it was the Communist intellectuals who sparked it.

What type of person was the Communist intellectual? How did he become a rebel? What enabled him to defy the central apparatus? These questions will be discussed in the following section, which will trace the main stages in the Communist intellectuals' evolution from orthodoxy to rebellion.

4

THE WRITERS'

REVOLT

The Soviet occupation of 1944–45 revolutionized the Hungarian literary scene as thoroughly as it did the political one. Not that the Communists tried to monopolize literary production. Though they immediately acquired decisive influence in cultural matters, they were careful to leave some scope of activity for non-Communists, as they did in the political sphere. As we have seen, however, the only non-Communists allowed to function in politics were those whom the Communists declared to be acceptable; that is, social-minded, progressive, and "democratic."[1] In directing cultural activities from behind the scenes, they used a similar procedure. On the one hand, a number of Communist authors, totally unfamiliar to the public or only dimly remembered from earlier times, were suddenly propelled into prominence as talents of the first magnitude. On the other hand, some well-known and popular writers whose outlook was deemed reactionary and antidemocratic, among them the playwright László Németh and the poet and translator of Shakespeare, Lörinc Szabó, were silenced altogether. The regime also refused to publish Lajos Kassák, a lifelong Socialist who had led a kind of proletarian avant-garde literary movement in the revolutionary year 1919.

Somewhere between the Communists and the ostracized "bourgeois" or socialist authors there were those whom the

Communists treated with benevolence even though they did not belong to the Party. Most of these, including Péter Veres and Gyula Illyés (the latter regarded by many as the outstanding literary figure of the period), represented a "populist" tendency; that is to say, they wrote from the viewpoint of the peasant, castigating the old regime's callousness toward him. The Communists had every reason to cultivate these writers and thus demonstrate the "alliance between the proletariat and the working peasantry." Similarly, generosity toward such "progressive" bourgeois writers as Jenö Heltai could serve as proof and illustration of the "alliance between the proletariat and the working intelligentsia." This broad-mindedness toward the progressive non-Party element was characteristic of Communist cultural policy during the coalition period, and to some extent even afterward. The "populist" writers, for example, continued to be published after the establishment of the one-party state.

The Communists were broad-minded also in their treatment of most of the outstanding writers of earlier generations, from such nineteenth-century classic figures as Sándor Petöfi and János Arany to the great poets of the early twentieth century, notably Endre Ady. With regard to these, as with the established writers of all nations, the standard Communist practice was to stress the "progressive" traits of their work, traits that made it possible to claim them as precursors of Marxism. With such literary figures as Goethe and Balzac, whose political views were conservative, this operation could not be performed without some extraordinary mental gymnastics (it was the Hungarian Marxist philosopher George Lukács who accomplished the feat in the most convincing fashion). With the Hungarian classics, however, the task was relatively easy; for the dominant Hungarian literary tradition is anti-authoritarian or even (as in the case of Petöfi and Ady) explicitly and vehemently revolutionary. In fact, the genuine anti-authoritarianism of the traditional classics turned out to be too much of a good thing for the Hungarian Communist leadership, since the people took to reading the hallowed texts as if they had been directed against *Communist* authoritarianism.

Classical authors and progressive non-Party writers, however, were only the outworks of Communist cultural policy. The inner bastion was manned by writers who were Party members. The writer in the Party was a peculiar phenomenon—a creator of imaginative works who at the same time was a functionary following instructions. This dual role (an uneasy and unstable one, since either function could be performed in the long run only at the expense of the other) was one that most of the Communist writers elected voluntarily, being convinced that there was no good art but that which served the people, and that the Party alone was competent to determine where the popular interest lay. The Communist writers revered the Party; they had a genuine admiration for everything Soviet, and most of them considered the regimentation of literature by the Party bureaucracy one of the distinctive marks of progressive humanity.

Among the writers, as among the political functionaries, it was the group of former *émigrés*, now back from Moscow, who occupied the highest positions. Among them were the playwright Gyula Háy, the philosopher George Lukács, and the essayist József Révai. Révai, a hard-line Stalinist, became one of the chief power-holders in the Hungarian Communist regime and remained very influential in ideological matters even after he was dropped from the Politburo at the beginning of the New Course in 1953; Háy and Lukács eventually joined the intra-Party opposition.

The *émigrés* were mostly older people whose loyalty to Communism dated back to the Russian Revolution of 1917. Most of them came from the cultivated Jewish middle class; their roots were in the pre–World War I socialist movement, whose radical offshoot, Bolshevism, they had joined under the impact of the war.

By the time these *émigré* writers returned to Hungary, their early enthusiasm for the Communist cause had become tempered by the years spent under Stalin, except for some out-and-out opportunists like Révai, to whom Stalinism was congenial. Another somewhat disillusioned member of this older generation of Communist writers was the novelist Tibor Déry, who had spent some time as an *émigré* in Western Europe. He, too, eventually came to play a prominent part in the writers' revolt.

The returning *émigrés*, however, represented only a thin upper crust among the Communist writers of Hungary. After the entry of the Soviet troops, large numbers of unknown young people suddenly burst into print, all fanatical Party men intent upon taking over Hungarian literature lock, stock, and barrel. They were brash, intolerant, impatient with the humanistic outlook of a Lukács and the disillusioned and somewhat ironical attitude of a Déry. Their background was varied; many were of middle-class Jewish origin, but there were also proletarian and peasant boys among them. Their reasons for adopting the Soviet creed had little in common with the largely altruistic motives for which the older generation (privileged as it was in its personal circumstances) had embraced socialism. These young men had personal scores to settle with the Horthy regime and with the Nazis, either because they were poor or because, being Jews, they had been savagely persecuted. (Hardly any of them had escaped the Nazi concentration camps, and all had lost near relatives.) The Soviet Union was their great rescuer and avenger. They sang its praises sincerely, with genuine hope.

Incidentally, they were lavishly rewarded. The Communists seemed to be insatiable in their demand for more and more popular literature, poetry, prose, and drama glorifying the bright new world. Any young man with a gift for phraseology who learned to master the simple technique of producing Party literature was assured of becoming a prominent person, a socially important figure, very unlike the poets and writers under the old order who, though sometimes buried with national honors, were seldom treated as important in their lifetime. In particular, to receive a high income from the state simply for writing poems was unheard of in pre-Communist Hungary. The Communists, however, showered bounty upon poets whose productions met the Party's specifications.

What were these specifications? The poems, to begin with, had to be simple—no modernism, no experimentation, no obscurity. Purely personal, subjective matters were unsuitable. In poetry—and, of course, in narrative works, drama, and essay literature as well—there was only one subject worthy of being treated: the Party and its mission. The task of the poet or the writer of prose was to invent new, stimulating variants of the basic theme of the contrast between Old and New—the haughty and wicked barons and capitalists of the old era maltreating the downtrodden people, the exploiters sent packing, and every simple working man and woman well looked after, happy, and proud in the new. This could be done easily enough with a modicum of talent; in fact, true talent was a liability rather than an asset, since it tempted the writer to stray from the simplicity of the basic idea. The best thing was to follow the canon of official Soviet literature: in poetry, rhymed prose would do; the profundity of the message need not go beyond such praiseworthy ideas as that "our Five-Year Plan must succeed"; and it could do no harm if praise for the Party and its leaders were laid on with a trowel.

The young poets and writers set to work with enormous zest. Those who could do no better than write rhymed prose or unrhymed bureaucratese fared best, because they produced exactly what the Party wanted. Quite a few of the young Communist writers, however, had genuine talent, notably the poets László Benjámin, Zoltán Zelk, and Péter Kuczka. In 1952, the chief literary commissar, Révai, mildly censured Benjámin and Zelk for writing unconventional poems filled with troubled, tragic accents, shocking in a socialist society.[2] There was more solicitude than hostility in Révai's strictures. (In fact, Zelk and Benjámin at that time still showed the most impeccable Party orthodoxy.) This incident merely illustrates the fact that, in a Communist regime, poetic imagery is a matter of state importance and is subject to constant governmental supervision. The few Communist authors who provoked serious objections from the Party's cultural commissars were members of the older generation, notably George Lukács and Tibor Déry. Déry's long novel *Felelet* (Answer) was vehemently denounced in 1952, because it presented the clandestine Hungarian Communist Party of the interwar period in a less than heroic light. The Writers' Association organized a debate on the book, and the Communist writers were instructed to attack Déry. They did as they were told; Déry had no defenders.[3]

The fact is that in 1952 none of the young Communist poets and writers who later turned rebels showed the slightest deviationist tendency. Minstrels of the regime, they poured forth with apparent relish the odes in honor of the hierarchy that they were obliged to write, as well as streams of vicious abuse against their own former friends, idealistic Communists like themselves, who had been tortured and broken by the new Inquisition. Several of the young writers later told me that in those days they had not yet begun to have serious doubts about the Party and their own role in their society. They were living within a closed system in which reasoning was possible only on the premises provided by the Party, even if these were totally at variance with personal experience. It took a long time for the younger intellectuals to shake off the Party's stranglehold over their thinking and their consciences; in most cases, the process of alienation did not start spontaneously. The first impetus toward a breach with the Party was furnished by the Party itself.

It was a shattering experience for the younger Communist

intellectuals when, in June 1952, the Central Committee denounced the policies the Party had followed up to then. The writers' main function had been to justify those policies to the public (and, in a sense, to posterity) as convincingly as possible. The June resolution, then, made short shrift of all their past endeavors, of their sense of mission as well as of their pride in achievement. Once the Party itself abandoned the position that they, the intellectuals, had been defending as the only historically correct one, their position became absurd. It was the more absurd since, ironically, the New Course proclaimed by the Central Committee appeared quite congenial to most of them, even though before June 1953 they would not have dared acknowledge any sympathy for what had then been labeled a "right deviation."

Political functionaries and bureaucrats were much less profoundly affected by the New Course, embarrassing as it was to many of them. They could (if pressed) switch over from a given policy line to one diametrically opposed, without feeling that this destroyed their self-image. Abrupt changes of line were part of the Communist bureaucrat's training; he was able to treat his own past record as irrelevant. The intellectual, however, was not. His whole being was summed up in his record, and the Party's devaluation of the earlier orthodoxy left him deflated and defenseless. This may be what one Communist writer had in mind when he said to me: "It is possible for a politician to change his tune on orders from above, but impossible for a writer. The writer wants to create something that is enduring; he needs continuity. We became rebels primarily because we felt that we could not exist as writers unless we ceased being conformists."

The interpretation of this statement is not a simple matter. It was not the prescribed change as such that went against the grain; nor was conformism as such difficult to accept as long as the New Course was in force. But in shifting to the New

Course, the writers realized, for the first time, that Party orthodoxy was not enough. To exist as writers, they had to adopt a position that was "enduring," one they could maintain once and for all. But this they could do only by acknowledging that the Party's official position was not the only yardstick of truth. It became necessary to develop independent standards, to judge things in terms of one's own experience. Many Communist writers reoriented themselves in this sense under the New Course, and thus entered upon the path that, by successive stages, led to outright rebellion.

It must be emphasized, however, that the Communist writers by no means repudiated their past *in toto* when they broke away from Party discipline and ceased to be loyal to the apparatus. They preserved continuity with their own past insofar as the general principles of Marxist socialism and the historical justification of the overthrow of the old social order were concerned. This, too, was important for the morale of the writers' opposition. Had they seen nothing but evil and error in their original adhesion to the Party, they would have lost the zest to act and fight. They did not turn against everything the Party and the movement stood for; they merely proclaimed that the Party had to be restored to the original purity of its intentions. Although intensely remorseful about their past betrayals, the Communist writers still cherished memories of the glorious dawn of the revolution, when to be a Communist meant to offer heroic, unstinting service to the cause, and brotherly solidarity prevailed among comrades.[4] As one writer told me, the tragedy was that the Party had achieved exclusive power. As soon as this happened, the idealistic purity of the era of opposition vanished; corruption and jealousy became prevalent, and the Party became a privileged group separated from the people.

The question, then, was how to recapture the original purity of the movement. Only if this were done could the intellectual still justify being a Communist, both to himself and to the people. An unregenerate Party had no defense whatever; a reformed Party, however, could and would become a legitimate spokesman of the masses—provided the reform was not delayed too long. The intellectuals were becoming aware of the enormous resentment the masses felt toward the Party. Their great fear was that the people would learn to hate everything connected with Communism, even the basic symbols of the movement; the intellectuals thus faced the problem of maintaining their identification with the ideal image of the Party without parting company with the people.

As time went on, it became more and more difficult for the Communist intelligentsia to preserve continuity, the integrity of its self-image. Under the New Course, the task of reforming the Party from within and of making amends for one's own aberrations looked relatively simple. But after the Party had turned against the New Course and its misdeeds became known in more vivid detail, the intellectuals were assailed by increasingly radical inner doubts, which corroded even the ideal image of the cause they were seeking to preserve. The most sensitive and guilt-ridden among them fell into black despair; some of the poems that will be quoted below reveal total bitterness. For these men, only revolt could offer some hope.

The following sections will deal with the main stages in the progressive alienation of the Communist intellectuals from their Party environment.

FROM SOCIAL CRITICISM TO ACTIVE INSUBORDINATION

The June 1953 resolution of the Central Committee of the Hungarian Communist Party impressed on the country's Communist writers that contemporary social arrangements, though they bore the Party's imprint, still called for criticism in the "progressive" vein; that is, the sort of criticism that, until then, had been applied only to the social iniquities of *past* systems. The new watchword was that Hungarian literature had to be revitalized by re-establishing contact with authentic, unembellished reality. The exclusive concern with conforming to the Party's wishes in the presentation of reality had made Hungarian literature dull and indigestible. To regain an audience, the writers had to study the life of the masses.[5]

This the writers began to do in the summer and fall of 1953, and not without a good deal of self-accusation. A typical expression of this mood was a poem entitled "Röpirat" (Leaflet) by the Communist poet István Simon. The language and style were the usual Party doggerel, but the content was new. "Up to now," the poet says, "I lived in high regions where I saw only splendor and happiness; my more favorable circumstances drew a veil over the harder life of others. I lived in the rapture of marvelous figures and fine achievements: I did not see how the excessive burden of work was breaking my people's back."[6]

The first notable product of the new critical realism was Péter Kuczka's "Nyírségi Napló" (Nyír County Diary).[7] This poem embellishes nothing: it depicts the desolate countryside of northeastern Hungary as an accursed landscape where nature is ungenerous and the people live in grim misery, for which they blame the Communist authorities. The main subject is the peasants' rising against the kolkhoz system following Nagy's inaugural speech.[8] When the kolkhoz peasants take a vote on the dissolution of the kolkhoz, hardly anyone votes to maintain it. A Party committee chairman complains: "There was nothing wrong here, we used to dance together all night; then there was that Nagy speech which drove the peasants crazy. They used to love me before, but now they spit on me, they come at me with pitchforks and clubs. Now tell me, Comrade, did I deserve this?" The final vignette shows an old woman shaking her fists at the sky and screeching imprecations against the Party.

The poem burst on the literary and political scene like a bombshell. Party bureaucrats condemned it indignantly, but the writers did not care; the leading literary periodicals (*Uj Hang* and *Csillag*) began publishing unorthodox, critical pieces. At this stage, the Communist authors were still cautious and moderate in making their points and drawing general conclusions. For one thing, the New Course, though reformist, was very much a Communist system, jealously guarding the Party's monopoly of political power. Thus it was possible and, from the Nagy government's point of view, essential to prod the Party's conscience from within and urge it to show greater consideration for the people; it was not possible to call the Party's role into question in radical fashion. For another, the Communist writers themselves, deeply disturbed though they were by the collapse of their earlier, Stalinist orientation, still clung to the hope that the New Course would cleanse the regime of its blemishes. Kuczka's poem ended on an optimistic note: in time, the Party would wipe away the desperate old woman's tears.

As time went on, however, it became more and more difficult for the Communist writers to identify themselves with the Party. It turned out that the critical June resolution of the Central Committee had failed to reveal fully the depravity of the Rákosi regime. The resolution had stated in a general way that many innocent people, including Party members, had suffered imprisonment because the authorities had violated the principles of legality. What had actually happened to these people, however, became clear to the intellectuals only when the victims, released and rehabilitated, turned up in Budapest and told their stories to their erstwhile friends. These confrontations plunged the Communist intellectuals into agonies of remorse and despair: the poems and articles they had written during the period of terror, applauding Rákosi and vilifying his victims, remained as monuments to their shame. Thereafter, remorse was a recurrent theme in the poetry of the younger generation of Communists.

65

"That's how we are, Sándor," Benjámin wrote in a poem addressed to his friend Sándor Haraszti.* "You were sent to hell by a lying accusation, and I am now addressing you from the hell of my guilt, since I had believed you guilty."[9]

Here are a few more samples of the same motif:

> If you let yourself go, horror engulfs you. If you try to defend yourself, the knife you wield spills your own blood. This is how I am choked by what I failed to do and also by what I did. I live in anxiety, caught up in other people's crimes without, in my own judgment within.[10]

> I shall get up. Maybe the sun will acknowledge me too as his son. . . . Maybe I can redeem myself, wash away my sins, if I find a task for myself.[11]

> Rather walk naked in the streets than don falsehood ever again![12]

In these poems, there is at least a glimmer of hope: by turning over a new leaf, one can redeem oneself. Others speak in more desperate accents, admitting that nothing can be salvaged from the collapse of faith and moral integrity the poets have experienced. "Don't see anything in me but the fragment of a soul that once was whole," Benjámin writes.[13] And again: "It makes no difference how long I shall drag on my existence—it will be of no use to anybody."[14] A poem by Tamás Aczél entitled "About Life" contains the following lines:

> Make amends for everything, with daring
> and resolution.
> Perhaps you will get out of the jungle,
> into the sun,
> You may then walk under trees, in a
> light breeze,

---

* Haraszti, sentenced to death as an accomplice of Rajk, had been saved from execution and was later released from prison.

All alone, unnoticed,
Outwardly free, inwardly sevenfold a
  prisoner.
Your loyal heart is asking: Yes? Answer!
Never—this is what I should answer
If I still could talk.[15]

Besides remorse and self-accusation, we find in the literary
output of the Communist rebels sharp attacks on the power
apparatus of the Party, particularly after the ouster of Nagy
and the liquidation of the New Course. The New Course allowed the writers to identify themselves with at least one seg-
ment of the official Party. Once the Nagy group had been condemned as deviationist, its intellectual supporters moved into
direct opposition. Benjámin wrote in 1955:

I have now learned that man may choose sorrow for joy's
sake, the hero may die for life's sake, but inhuman for humanity's sake, dishonorable for honor's sake, mendacious for
truth's sake, no woman's son can ever be.[16]

ORGANIZED OPPOSITION

After the liquidation of the New Course, the Party organization within the Writers' Association became an organized
nucleus of intra-Party opposition. "At first," a leading member
of the group, the novelist Tamás Aczél, told me, "we were sending up warning reports through channels: we tried to acquaint
the leadership with the mood prevailing in the country." This
form of loyal opposition, however, was of no avail. Far from
appreciating the writers' warnings, the Party leadership resorted to repression. An issue of *Irodalmi Ujság* was seized and
the editor, George Hámos, dismissed; some independent-minded members of the staff of the Party daily *Szabad Nép* were removed also.

The writers now went over to the attack. On October 18,

67

1955, the most prominent members of the Writers' Association sent the Central Committee a memorandum protesting against these and other "brutal" interventions in cultural life, including the banning of Imre Madách's *The Tragedy of Man,* a national classic. The memorandum pointed out that ever since the Central Committee's resolution of June 1953, which guaranteed the independence of cultural work, all measures of this sort had been illegal; in fact, not only the Third Party Congress of May 1954 but also the Central Committee's resolution of March 1955 (which condemned Nagy and liquidated the New Course) still fully upheld those decisions concerning cultural life. And the memorandum concluded:

> We respectfully ask the Central Committee to ensure compliance with the resolutions of the Central Committee and of the Party Congress so as to suppress the antidemocratic methods by which organs and functionaries conduct affairs, methods that disfigure the Party's cultural policy, paralyze our intellectual life, and undermine the Party's prestige and influence; we also urge the Committee to reconsider the abusive administrative measures and guarantee the writers, journalists, and other intellectual workers a climate of Communist frankness and honesty or, in other words, the opportunity to produce without disturbance creative works capable of serving the cause of the people and of Socialism.[17]

The Communist Party cell of the Writers' Association, meeting on November 10, endorsed the memorandum; several speakers at the meeting vehemently attacked the regime.[18]

Stung to the quick, the Politburo struck back. The Central Committee meeting in December stigmatized the writers' actions as seditious, and the signatories of the memorandum (about sixty in number[19]) were put under the strongest pressure to withdraw their signatures. The majority did, but not so the most prominent ones, including Háy, Déry, and Aczél. This open rebellion created an enormous scandal in the Party. In December, the unrepentant writers were called before a plenary session of the Budapest Party "activists" and were treated to long speeches of vilification amidst the howls of an enraged mob of five thousand. The leaders of the writers' opposition expected arrest; they burned their papers and slept in friends' apartments. No police measures were taken, however. Some time after the December meeting, Rákosi called Tamás Aczél on the telephone and asked him whether he needed any money or would accept some other favor. But Aczél held firm.[20]

I asked several members of the writers' group how it was possible for the opposition to capture press organs published under Party auspices. The explanation was that the rebels simply used their official authority as the Party's appointed functionaries. "The Agitprop branch," one of the writers said, "had made a tactical mistake. They did not know that we had ceased to be loyal Communists and appointed us to key posts in the Association." During the hullabaloo about *Irodalmi Ujság's* opposition campaign, the government tried to kill the paper by withdrawing its newsprint allowance. The head of the publishing trust, however, was furious. "The paper is now making money for the first time," he is reported to have said. "The state cannot close down an enterprise that is showing a profit."[21] Even after provoking an open conflict with the leadership, the writers, protected by organizational inertia and informal backing at various levels, retained a foothold within the apparatus. Still, they could not be sure that they would not be crushed. The winter of 1955–56 was an uneasy one for them.

The turning point came at the end of February, with the Twentieth Congress of the Communist Party of the Soviet Union. Khrushchev's speech denouncing Stalin's misdeeds and the Congress resolutions condemning the "cult of personality" created an entirely new situation in the Hungarian Party. The last defenses of orthodoxy crumbled. Before the Twentieth Congress, the moral issue raised by the purges had not been entirely clear-cut. Protests against the outrages visited upon innocent and loyal Party members could still be dismissed as being inspired only by "bourgeois," "individual" morality, as opposed to true, proletarian ethics, which justified anything that strengthened the Communist movement. For the Communist intellectuals, uneasy about their own "bourgeois" background, this argument had carried considerable persuasive force. Now, however, Khrushchev was saying that Stalin's personal tyranny had actually *weakened* the Party; hence, he was condemning the policy of terroristic purges even in terms of this "Marxist," "proletarian" criterion.[22] In making this point, the Soviet Party seemed to have declared open season on Rákosi and his clique, and the opposition was not slow in making use of this opening.

The trickle of writings attacking the regime became a flood. *Irodalmi Ujság*, which had turned into a full-fledged opposition organ, acquired enormous popularity in this new guise. The Petőfi Circle started its campaign. From then on, the opposition was on the offensive. Within a few months, the whole authority structure of the Party was corroded. Thus undermined from within, the regime was not able to withstand the onslaught of the masses in the October days.

5

THE

DISINTEGRATION

OF AUTHORITY

RÁKOSI UNDER ATTACK

Rákosi does not seem to have sensed the danger to his position. As an ex-Communist functionary told me, the Communist leader appeared unruffled when he returned from the Twentieth Congress. He told his friends not to worry: "In a few months, Khrushchev will be the traitor and everything will be back to normal." As it turned out, however, the situation in the Hungarian Party became increasingly abnormal.

At a Party meeting shortly after the Congress, an obscure functionary of one of the Budapest district organizations introduced a motion calling for Rákosi's resignation. The man expected to be arrested, but the police did not touch him; instead, he became a minor celebrity. From then on, the proletarian members of Party district organizations began to speak out; some of them made drastic attacks upon Rákosi at Party meetings.[1]

In *Irodalmi Ujság* of May 5, Gyula Háy delivered a frontal assault:

> The cult of personality has contaminated all of our literature. There is perhaps not a single one among us who has not, at least temporarily, confused enthusiasm for the great cause with infatuation with certain personalities. . . . One

71

of the most important immediate tasks of our Writers' Association is to help all writers of good will to free themselves of this contamination. . . . We know that literature does not live in isolation. Should there be no radical change in our public, political, and economic life under the sign of the Twentieth Congress, the most beautiful literary resolution would be useless. But do we have a right to suppose that there will be no such changes in the political and economic life of our country? The influence of the Twentieth Congress, the grandiose upsurge of humanity, the great triumph of human dignity, will not and cannot stop at our frontiers, they cannot bypass our country. This is why we firmly believe in a better future for our literature, and as we believe in it, we are also struggling for it.

This was too much for the Old Guard; Sándor Gergely, one of the few writers who remained loyal to Rákosi, wrote a reply to Háy which *Irodalmi Ujság* magnanimously printed on May 19. "Could the reader not easily be induced to think," Gergely asked, "that those who expect a radical change in the country's economic and political life mean by this the liquidation of the dictatorship of the proletariat . . . and the restoration of bourgeois rule?" This was a clear warning: if the opposition writers continued in this vein, they could easily be accused of being imperialist agents plotting the overthrow of the dictatorship of the proletariat. In the spring of 1956, however, the writers were not to be intimidated. They thought that the spirit of the Twentieth Congress was protecting them. Indeed, no police measures were taken even after the most extreme attacks. The young Communist writer Sándor Lukácsi, for example, called Rákosi "Judas" at a cell meeting of the Writers' Association; but he was merely expelled from the Party.

The most explosive incident of the writers' campaign was the Petőfi Circle's meeting of June 27, devoted to "Questions of Information and the Press." Several writers, notably Tibor Déry and Tibor Tardos, attacked the regime with unprecedented vehemence before a crowd of six thousand that spilled over into the street. The debate lasted from 6:30 P.M. until 4:00 A.M. Three members of the Central Committee were present: Déry attacked them mercilessly to their face: "these [József Révai, József Darvas, Márton Horváth] were the ones who had imposed the rule of terror over the mind." Losonczy, who spoke last, made a eulogy of Nagy that was much applauded.[2]

The Central Committee was thoroughly alarmed by the tone of the meeting and by the Poznan uprising which broke out on the following day. Meeting hurriedly on June 30, the Committee decided to take drastic measures. The Petöfi Circle was dissolved and numerous intellectuals were expelled from the Party, including, of course, all the organizers of the writers' opposition. The momentum of the opposition movement, however, was not checked. Such purely disciplinary measures as expulsion from the Party no longer had any effect whatever. Only arrests could have silenced the opposition, but Rákosi was not able to use this weapon. He was losing the struggle waged on the intellectual and organizational level: within three weeks after the Petöfi Circle meeting he was deposed.

RÁKOSI'S FALL

Why was Rákosi not in a position to subdue the intra-Party opposition by police methods? To begin with, Moscow had banned the use of police measures against Party members. But we must also consider the conditions prevailing in the Communist police apparatus itself. As we have mentioned,[3] the New Course of 1953 with its emphasis upon "legality," together with Beria's liquidation, had set the stage for a wave of persecutions against the former persecutors themselves. These purges had a profoundly demoralizing effect upon the police. Obviously, the Party leaders' maneuver was totally dishonest. The police chiefs were presented as having practiced terrorism on their own initiative, as independent policy-makers, although in fact they had always acted on instruction from the political leadership, and they understandably resented being thus made scapegoats for the sins of the politicians. But, in addition, the purges of the police officers demonstrated how risky it was to proceed against one category of Party member on behalf of another. The police, therefore, became reluctant to depart from the general policy line banning terror within the Party, and would not take action even when confronted with open rebellion that in earlier times would have entailed automatic police intervention.

In Hungary, the police problem was particularly acute, because the synthetic trials of the Rajk group and many others, organized by Rákosi from 1949 on, constituted the most explosive issue in the opposition's campaign against him. Rákosi saw that the authority of the regime would be hopelessly compromised if the whole truth were told in public. After all, the surviving victims who were Party members and fellow-travelers had been freed and rehabilitated. Why not leave things at that? Why bring up the fateful question of responsibility? The opposition, however, insisted precisely on this. It held that it was not enough for the chief culprit, Rákosi, magnanimously to offer to let bygones be bygones. He had to account for his actions and tell the country how and why things happened as they did. And, most important, Rajk and his co-victims who had been unjustly executed had to be rehabilitated too. Julia Rajk, László's widow, who had been released from prison, was ceaselessly campaigning for this behind the scenes, and also spoke publicly to the same effect at a Petöfi Circle meeting.

Very much against his will, Rákosi made the desired declaration in a speech at Eger on March 29. The Party, he said, had ordered an investigation of the cases of Rajk and other Communists or Socialists sentenced in the purges, and it had turned out that all were victims of "provocation." The police had "misled" the government. Those responsible, that is, Péter and his collaborators, had already been unmasked and sentenced the year before.

Rákosi's evasion of responsibility, the hypocrisy of his explanation, only added to the general indignation against him; people in Budapest referred to him as "the murderer," or "the bald-headed murderer."[4] The police, too, were enraged. When Rákosi addressed the annual meeting of the highest echelon of AVH officers in June 1956, he was booed. A high-ranking member of the police force reportedly told him to his face that his conduct had "reached the lowest point to which political morality could sink."[5]

Had it been possible for Rákosi at this point to resort to terrorism, he could have saved his position. As things were, however, his nominal control of the apparatus was not enough to save him. The fact that his record made him a target for daily attacks that could not be silenced turned him into a liability for the Party. The potential dangers inherent in continued agitation were vividly brought home to the leadership by the Poznan uprising of June 28. This showed that mass rebellion was a definite possibility. How to stop political agitation now became the foremost problem for the Party. Silencing the Petöfi Circle was not enough; it was only too clear that renewed defiance had to be expected from the disaffected Party intelligentsia as long as Rákosi remained leader of the Party. The subleaders, notably Gerö, seeing that only Rákosi's withdrawal could restore quiet in the Party, tried to persuade him to go. Rákosi, however, desperately clung to his position, arguing that if he quit under fire, the whole edifice of Communist power in Hungary would crumble. To save himself, he reportedly intended to order mass arrests; his list of four hundred people to be arrested included Nagy and the chief rebels of the Petöfi Circle.[6] The Moscow center, however, would not tolerate such action. To allow Rákosi to purge his opponents would have been ruinous to the Soviet policy of *rapprochement* with Tito, apart from the explosive consequences it might have had in Hungary.

It was Mikoyan who took matters in hand. He flew to Budapest in mid-July and told the Hungarians that Rákosi had to go. At the Central Committee meeting called to rule on this matter, Rákosi is reported to have fought the decision tooth and nail, arguing that the situation could be saved only if the disparate elements in the Party were made to cooperate. János Kádár, however, declared that this was impossible: "There are mountains of corpses between us."[7] Mikoyan, too, remained adamant. On July 18, Rákosi finally handed in his resignation and left by plane for Russia.

THE FINAL STAGE

Rákosi's removal failed to put an end to political agitation. His successor as First Secretary of the Party was Ernö Gerö, the Old Guard's No. 2 man who had been closely associated with Rákosi's basic policies (police terror, overindustrialization, and collectivization) and with the liquidation of the New Course. Gerö's appointment was not calculated to disarm the opposition, which wanted above all the restoration and strengthening of the New Course and the recall of Nagy. Such a radical reorientation, however, was out of the question for the apparatus, and the Moscow center, too, maintained its veto upon Nagy and the New Course. Both Gerö and his Soviet superiors considered it best to make concessions slowly and gradually. While warning against impetuous changes that could only render the situation still more unstable, Gerö promised reforms in reasonable time. He treated the opposition with kid gloves. The expulsion from the Party of the rebels of the Petöfi Circle, with the exception of Déry and Tardos, was revoked, and the Circle itself was able to resume its activities in September. Gerö also made cautious attempts to broaden the political basis of the regime by offering government positions to a number of non-Communists.[8] Placating the opposition in this way appeared to him preferable to handing the reins of power to Nagy and his group, since his proposed method of broadening the government at least would have left intact the distribution of power *within* the Party. But Gerö's "rescue action," as it was called, petered out: his offers had no takers.

Meanwhile, the literary campaign went on, more vehement than ever. In August and September, Gyula Háy, Tamás Aczél, and a woman journalist, Judith Máriássy, published a number of articles in *Irodalmi Ujság* and elsewhere, describing the luxurious life of big Party functionaries. These articles caused an enormous sensation. The apparatus, scorned and held up to ridicule, was helpless, for it had become utterly impossible to intimidate the opposition. The Writers' Association, at its congress of September 17–18, filled all leading positions with Communist rebels and with socialist and even bourgeois writers who had once been ostracized or imprisoned by the regime.

During the early autumn, with the sands running out, Gerö continued his desperate maneuvering. On October 6, an astonishing spectacle took place: Rajk and some of his co-victims were reburied in a solemn state funeral attended by 200,000 people. The initiative came from Julia Rajk and a number of former purge victims. After rather difficult negotiations, the regime finally authorized the rite and, taking its cue from Rákosi's original maneuver, managed to turn it into a demonstration against the political police. No AVH men were present to watch over the crowd; instead, order was maintained by high military officers. The atmosphere was tense, but there were no disturbances. After the funeral, a group of students marched to the statue of Count Batthyány, who had been executed by the Austrians on October 6, 1849, and deposited a wreath. There was, of course, no interference from the police.[9]

A few days later, Mihály Farkas, once a close collaborator of Rákosi and one of the chief terrorists of the purge period, was arrested. This showed the increased influence of Kádár, Losonczy, and other purge victims within the government: they were now able to take revenge. But Farkas's arrest had as little power to save Gerö as Strafford's execution to save Charles I.

The Old Guard was giving ground step by step. Feelers had

been put out to Nagy before; reportedly, the Russians had come to favor his return to political life, and now began to cultivate him. The new Soviet ambassador, Yuri V. Andropov, invited him for a friendly talk in his office; Mikoyan, passing through Budapest once more, sought him out and was demonstratively amiable.[10] On October 4, Nagy wrote a letter to the Central Committee asking that his case be reconsidered; he suggested that if readmitted he would be available for a political position, provided he was given a task compatible with his convictions, his Marxist-Leninist principles, and his personal honor.[11]

On October 13, the Politburo replied to the letter, restoring Nagy's Party membership and putting the blame for his expulsion on the deposed Rákosi. But the reply also indicated that Nagy's future in the Party still depended on his acknowledging his earlier political mistakes. Clearly, the Party was not yet in a mood to give free rein to Nagy and his "Marxist-Leninist principles," in other words, his NEP policy. Yet, as subsequent events showed, Nagy's reappointment at this moment probably would have forestalled the revolution, for the masses had confidence in him. Had he been at the head of the government from mid-October on, it is safe to assume that any mass demonstration that did break out would have taken a far less hostile turn.

During the final stage, both sides in the intra-Party struggle were looking to the masses, and to the industrial workers in particular. It was generally felt, especially after Poznan, that the further course of events depended on whether the workers were stirred to action by the opposition or, on the contrary, pacified by the government. In the summer, both sides tried to establish direct contact with the workers. Prime Minister András Hegedüs visited the Csepel factories in June, but apparently only handpicked workers were permitted to see him.[12] The writers also began to talk to workers in the factories at about this time, sensing that action by the industrial workers, rather than ferment in the urban intelligentsia, might have decisive political consequences.

The workers' response, however, was far less enthusiastic than the writers had expected. As one of the writers told me, it was very difficult to establish contact; for the workers were deeply suspicious of all members of the Communist upper crust. Things were not made easier by the fact that the writers neither could nor would attack the Party and Communism as such, but were merely pleading for reforms (radical ones, to be sure) within the framework of the system. This drew no warm response from the workers, who had long lost any hope that the system could change its spots. In fact, their defeatism made them doubt whether there was any possibility of successful action to improve conditions so long as the political police were in the background. An old Csepel worker summed up the situation in the slang phrase *"Sóherek a prolik"*—"the proletarians are strictly from hunger." As we shall see when we come to the "mass pattern" of the revolution, this defeatist attitude underwent little change until the October uprising.

THE STUDENTS' REBELLION

The opposition was thus unsuccessful in its attempt to enlist mass support for its campaign against the Old Guard. In the end, admittedly, it was a violent mass outburst in Budapest that gave events a decisive turn, but this mass action was neither organized nor even directly inspired by the intra-Party opposition. Its origin was fortuitous: a clash between the police and street crowds attracted by a student demonstration.

We may consider this student demonstration as the point of juncture between the "elite pattern" and the "mass pattern" of the Hungarian Revolution. The intra-Party opposition was not able to stir up the masses, because it restricted itself to verbal manifestations and because its main concern—restoring the Party to moral and ideological purity—did not affect the masses very deeply. The students' demonstration, however, set the masses in motion by providing a physical stimulus and an emotional appeal. It triggered an unplanned and unforeseeable chain reaction.

In itself, the students' action was part of the "elite pattern," since it started from an organizational basis provided by the regime. Not being "insiders" like the Communist writers, the students had no power within the apparatus, but as members of the Communist League of Working Youth (the DISZ) they at least had legitimate organizational channels through which they could operate. Initiative from below was possible in the DISZ, which was only loosely controlled by the Party apparatus; as we have seen, the opposition writers had succeeded in infiltrating it to the extent of capturing control of the Petőfi Circle. In the autumn of 1956, the students simply seceded from the DISZ, which let them go without much ado. In October, the student body of the University of Szeged announced the formation of an independent student organization; the other universities followed suit.

This organizational step was a revolutionary act; it meant that the students were shaking off the tutelage of the regime's control organs, since the Party had no voice in the independent student associations. The authorities, however, did not interfere. A wholesale procedure against the students was indeed out of the question. It was vital for the regime to maintain the fiction that students as a body were loyal. Moreover, the authorities may have hoped that the new student organizations would remain nonpolitical and devote themselves to academic and social welfare activities.

As it turned out, no sooner were the student organizations born than they plunged into the thick of national politics. The first act of the independent student associations of Budapest was to call mass meetings of students not in order to discuss student matters, but to debate the problems and grievances of the nation. The feeling that big political changes were imminent was in the air; in Poland, the intra-Party opposition, backed by the aroused masses, had just successfully defied the Soviet leaders in a bold bid for national independence and social justice. To the students, it was unthinkable that Hungary should not follow suit. They flocked together in drafting committees, trying to formulate a set of national demands to be carried by the plenary meetings; these, then, would be broadcast to the world. The demands were clearly inspired by the events in Poland: they stressed reform within the Party, action against the most badly compromised members of the Old Guard, and greater equality in Soviet-Hungarian relations.

Like the writers' campaign, the students' action was confined to nonviolent, verbal manifestations against the existing order, and restricted itself to using legitimate organizational bases and communication channels. To this extent, the students' initiative was intrinsic to the elite pattern of the revolution: it was an attack from within the Communist power system, and, moreover, one that stopped short of any direct physical clash with the apparatus.

Yet the students were much further from the center of power than the writers or the bureaucrats who had carried on opposition from the inside. In many respects, the students belonged to the mass, and, in the revolution, their action was to display some of the characteristics of mass behavior. For example, they had not been engaged in continuous, chronic defiance; like the mass, they made a sudden jump from seeming discipline and quiescence to overt insubordination. Also, there was in the students' antigovernment behavior no trace of an appeal to a higher Party authority against the elements they were combating; approval or disapproval from *any* authority seemed to be a matter of complete indifference to them. This indifference indicated alienation from the Party of the same kind, if not as extreme in degree, as that of the masses. Finally, to mention one more point, the students' behavior reflected no intense struggles of conscience such as the writers had gone through. They did not feel responsible for the regime and were not tormented by the need to redeem themselves before their own consciences, the people, or history.

The students planned a peaceful demonstration. They were careful to seek official permission to hold it, and after some difficulty this was finally granted. Indeed, the students' parade on October 23 was peaceful and well-behaved enough, but the crowds it attracted became more and more agitated. The crowd's insistence upon having the students' demands put on the air, and the radio authorities' stubborn refusal to do so, finally led to a violent clash in which a new pattern of revolutionary behavior, the mass pattern, came to the fore.

6

SUBMISSION

AND

INSUBORDINATION

INSUBORDINATION IN THE ELITE AND IN THE MASS

One of the salient differences between elite and mass behavior *before* the revolution was that in most occupational categories non-Party elements were more passive, less ready to engage in open criticism and other antiregime activities, than disaffected Communist insiders.

The writers' opposition, for example, was almost exclusively a Party affair. One of the leaders of the movement told me that those Hungarian writers who did not belong to the Party maintained complete reserve during the crucial early stages of the campaign. The non-Party group included the old Hungarian authors of established reputation. These writers, some of whom had belonged to the political Right under the old regime, fully sympathized with the aims of the opposition, but they were too vulnerable to assume any active political role. Only during the last few weeks before the revolution, when the disintegration of the regime was far advanced, did they begin to add their voice to the chorus of opposition.

Among students, the situation seems to have been similar. Former students of middle-class origin told me that they felt very insecure because of their anomalous position and hence refrained from making any political remarks in public. Although the Communists had laid down the rule that only young people of worker and peasant origin could be admitted to higher studies, many young people who did not meet this requirement had managed to enter the university by giving misleading answers about their class of origin in the questionnaires they had to fill out. In order to avoid trouble, they had to study hard and remain inconspicuous. Students of working-class or peasant background, on the other hand, were encouraged to be politically articulate. In the early times, they often paraded an aggressive Marxism; later, as they became more and more disillusioned, they were the ones most likely to make critical comments at Party-sponsored student meetings.

In the industrial sector, Communist control of the labor force was complete, and the workers' discontent could not find open expression. The workers in the plants, on the whole, refrained from demonstrations of any kind. In Communist Party organizations, however, working-class members began to speak up in the spring of 1956, after the Twentieth Congress of the CPSU; this was the first articulate criticism to come from the ranks of industrial labor.

DIFFERENT DEGREES OF "ATOMIZATION" IN THE MASS

Before the revolution, open expression of antiregime feelings in the mass varied strikingly in frequency and kind from one group to another. At one end of the scale, we find white-collar office workers. From the interview material that I collected or that was made available to me by the Columbia University Project, it appears that this was the most thoroughly "atomized" and intimidated group in Hungary.* Among its members there seems to have been little, if any, communication of antiregime

* "Atomization" refers here to the extent to which people refrain from expressing their true feelings about political matters.

84

feelings, even in small private groups. A girl typist, for example, who had been employed in a big state trust, told me that one could not talk politics even to one's own brother. Asked whether there had been any change as time went on, she denied this categorically and maintained that there had been no noticeable relaxation until the moment of the revolution. The atmosphere she described seems to have been typical of the clerical employee group.

Among industrial workers, atomization appears to have been only slightly less strong and pervasive. As we have seen, the opposition writers when they tried to stir up the factory workers found them unresponsive and skeptical.[1] Some contemporary reports—articles and letters written by workers and published in *Irodalmi Ujság* in the summer and fall of 1956—present a similar picture. Thus, the trade unionist Emil Horn, writing in the issue of June 23, stated that the Twentieth Congress of the CPSU had found little response among the workers, who were apathetic and tired of politics. Commenting on this statement, a Csepel worker wrote in the issue of June 30: "It must be admitted that the workers do not believe in fine words unsupported by tangible acts. They do not look at things from above. They base their judgments solely on actual changes that they experience themselves."

Interviews with workers (both those I collected and those contained in the Columbia series) show little awareness even of the genuine changes that took place under the New Course. There are references to some improvement between 1953 and 1955, but this is mostly described as insignificant as well as transient. The interviews also contain direct evidence of high atomization. Replying to questions about the possibility of critical talk, most workers denied that it existed except in intimate circles; and even close friends tended to avoid general topics and to center their complaints on personal difficulties and on facts, rather than discuss the political and institutional aspects of things. In the presence of strangers, they would say nothing at all.

In a letter to the editor of *Irodalmi Ujság* published as late as October 13, 1956, the "atomized" pattern of behavior was described as still prevalent among Csepel workers:

> At Csepel as elsewhere, people's attitudes are still guided by the adage, "Keep your mouth shut and you'll have no headaches." Let's take an everyday example from the factory. Some workers around a lathe talk about such questions as whether Imre Nagy will agree to make his self-criticism, why Tito could go to the Crimea, whether there will be a wage adjustment on January 1, and so on. Then a Party functionary approaches, and everybody starts talking about the football pool.

Atomization appears from the interviews to have been most thorough in large industrial plants, where the labor force was inflated by fresh recruits from the peasantry and the Communists had a strong apparatus of supervisors and informers. It was much less so in small plants that had retained their old personnel—organized workers who had been with them for many years. As far as they could, these men kept alive the old Social Democratic and trade union traditions of political consciousness. Among unskilled laborers, a group that included many *déclassé* elements who had formerly belonged to high-status groups, communication of political feelings was often relatively uninhibited; these people had little to lose and sometimes were less strictly supervised than the skilled workers in big plants.

It is in interviews with members of the intelligentsia that one hears time and again about a consistent uninhibited exchange of political comments not only in private gatherings but also among colleagues. Typical are such statements as "I never made any secret of my political feelings"; "Among colleagues, we always talked freely"; and "We talked even in the presence of our Communist colleagues and were confident that they would not report on us." On the question of talking politics with strangers, the typical intellectual's opinion was that this was a matter of psychological insight, a kind of sixth sense one learned to trust. There were ways of sizing up the stranger. One informant said that he once visited a bar with a man he did not know at all; when the stranger ordered a highball (rather than vodka), he knew he could trust him.

In order to check my impression about the different degree of atomization among intellectuals and workers, respectively, I made a breakdown (see table) of the relevant answers in 101 interviews prepared by the Columbia University Project on Hungary. Of the respondents, 71 came from the middle class or intelligentsia, and 30 were of working-class origin. The answers tabulated referred to questions about the possibility of discussing political subjects, and were divided into three categories: "high atomization," "neutral," and "low atomization." The "high" answers stressed the impossibility or dangerous nature of such discussions, the pervasive mutual fear among work associates, the necessity of constant self-control, and so on; the "low" respondents reported free communication among workers, little fear of denunciation, the possibility of guessing who was trustworthy, and the like. The "neutral" answers fell between these extremes, with such qualifications as that discussion was not invariably dangerous but was possible, for instance, with friends of long standing or among family members.

ATOMIZATION AMONG INTELLECTUALS AND WORKERS

	Respondents' Origin	
Answers	Upper Class	Lower Class
High	25 (35%)	18 (60%)
Neutral	20 (28%)	5 (17%)
Low	26 (37%)	7 (23%)
Total	71 (100%)	30 (100%)

The difference between the upper- and the lower-class pattern becomes even more striking if we eliminate from the "high" upper-class group eight respondents who were *déclassé* elements forced to do menial work and three others who were clerical workers in government offices. Three more were children of school age. If we eliminate these fourteen cases, only eleven (19 per cent) "high" upper-class respondents remain; these were people who did professional work in offices or institutions in which Party controls were particularly intense and oppressive.

Interviews with school children reveal some mutual distrust and avoidance of political topics, but it appears that the "upper-class" pattern of relatively uninhibited talk about political matters was far more prevalent in this group, regardless of the children's social class. I talked to a number of young people about their school experiences; several reported that children were in the habit of putting embarrassing political questions to the teacher or contradicting his obligatory propagandistic statements. Most children apparently reacted to Communist indoctrination with firm rejection; it clashed too much with what they could see for themselves. With their peers, however, they showed relatively little interest in talking politics; for the Communist variety was distasteful, and knowledge about other political systems or ideas was unobtainable. Among lower-class children, in particular, sports seem to have been by far the most attractive general topic of conversation.

At the opposite end from the office workers on the scale of antiregime activity we find the peasantry, the one class that the Communists, in spite of extraordinary efforts, never succeeded in putting under control. The Communists' aim was to put all of Hungary's agriculture on a cooperative basis, and they used every means of pressure to force each of the country's one-and-a-half million independent farmers to sign over his land to a "productive cooperative" (kolkhoz) and then enter the kolkhoz as a member. Those who were recalcitrant were systematically hounded out of business; they were assessed for taxes impossible to pay, fined on every pretext, imprisoned on trumped-up charges.[2] One peasant gave me an illustration of these methods: A decree was issued obliging each peasant always to keep a barrel full of water on his farm to be available in case of fire. During the night, a policeman would come around and let the water out of the barrel. The next day he would come back and note the offense, and the peasant would be fined. The harassment was such that it seemed impossible to withstand it for long. Joining the kolkhoz, on the other hand, meant lower taxes, the end of harassment, a measure of official favor. Yet many peasants held on to their land against impossible odds. They met exorbitant delivery quotas and paid enormous taxes and fines, totally exhausting themselves in the process, just to be "their own masters" and call a piece of land their own. Very often, continued refusal to sign up led to imprisonment, but many peasants preferred even that to capitulation. A minority of the peasants (mostly former agricultural workers who were susceptible to Communist propaganda) joined the kolkhozes voluntarily, but the vast majority either remained independent to the end or signed up only after they had exhausted every possibility of resistance.

Rákosi's collectivization drive reached its peak in December 1952; at that time, the land holdings of the kolkhozes totaled 1,404,000 hectares, or 26 per cent of Hungary's 5,400,000 hectares of arable land. An additional 700,000 hectares belonged to "state farms," corresponding to the Russian sovkhozes. Thus, more than one-third of Hungary's arable land had been transferred to the "socialist sector." By December 1952, Hungary's 5,315 kolkhozes had 515,000 active members.[3] Numerically, therefore, the success of four years of intensive socialization was not negligible, but it had been obtained at an enormous cost in terms of productivity. The collective sector was much less productive than the private one.

There were several reasons for this. For one thing, the kolkhozes were strictly bound to observe production plans laid down by the central authorities. This led to many crop failures, because the central authorities were not aware of local conditions and often insisted on programs for which the local soil and climate were unsuitable. Furthermore, mechanization, which in theory was bound to ensure the superiority of large-scale collective farming over small-scale private farming, was by no means an unmixed blessing in practice. Defective machines caused enormous losses; the big combines foisted upon the collective farms often compressed the soil to such an extent that the seeds could not develop properly.[4] Finally, and most important, the peasant lacked motivation to achieve high output on kolkhoz land. Working his own land, he gave his all to producing as much as possible; pressed into a collective, he saw his interest in working as little as possible.

As the collectivization campaign went on, even private farmers began to lose their zest for production. They had no incentive to improve their land, knowing that it might be taken away from them at any time. It became apparent that Hungary's growing urban population could not be fed unless the private farmers' incentive were restored. To restore it was one of the main objectives of Nagy's New Course.

As we have seen, the Party apparatus did everything in its power to prevent the large-scale dismantling of cooperatives. Nevertheless, the peasants' anti-kolkhoz drive, authorized by Nagy, achieved considerable success. Between October and December 1953, the kolkhozes lost about one-half their membership. At the same time, however, the land holdings of the cooperatives were reduced by only about 20 per cent.[5] The Communists apparently saw to it that the farmers "choosing freedom" could take only a minimum of land with them; yet a substantial part of the kolkhoz membership was willing to regain independence even at this price. Being left short of workers, the cooperatives in 1954 began leasing land to private farmers on a sharecropping basis.[6]

Submission and Insubordination

After the storm of 1953, the regime tried to stimulate *voluntary* enrollment in the cooperatives by offering new members material inducements such as tax privileges, but this campaign had very little effect.[7] The institutional setting of the collective farm, with its bureaucratic patterns of authority and management, proved utterly unpalatable to formerly independent peasants, whose life interest had been centered on attaining the status that went with personal ownership of land, and on exercising independent management functions. (It was easier for the formerly landless to adapt themselves to the kolkhoz setting.) Given freedom of action, the majority of the collectivized peasantry attempted a return to private farming. This happened first during the early New Course period of 1953, in the teeth of heavy pressure from the Party, and again, with less interference from the Communist authorities, during the revolutionary October days of 1956. When the revolution was over, the majority of the "socialized" farms had been dissolved, and the Kádár regime, installed in power after the military reconquest of Hungary, had to start virtually from scratch in restoring collectivized agriculture. At the beginning of 1957, it was announced that the collective farms still in existence, or restored after the revolution, numbered only 1,599, as compared to more than 5,000 before the revolution.[8]

7

POLITICAL CONTROL

AND INSTITUTIONAL

ENVIRONMENT

CULTURAL DETERMINANTS OF POLITICAL BEHAVIOR

The differences in the pre-revolutionary political behavior of the various social groups in Hungary may be traced back, in part, to the different characteristics of their cultural background, as well as to certain permanent group goals. Thus, if middle-class members were more articulate about politics than the small employees and the workers, this was due, in part, to their greater need for and skill in expressing their political opinions. Talking politics had always been one of the favorite pastimes of the Hungarian middle class, and it was not abandoned even when it became risky. The peasants' behavior, in turn, reflected their unvarying pursuit of one supreme goal: independent existence as producers in a market economy. They stubbornly clung to this under the greatest pressure and never accepted any substitute. The peasantry's case, however, was unique; none of the other classes was able to maintain the continuity of its traditional political behavior. The proletariat, to be sure, was encouraged by the Communists to assert its class identity and class consciousness, but at the same time it was deprived of every possibility of pursuing such traditional class goals as higher wages and shorter working hours. The former upper and middle groups were either totally uprooted or thoroughly shaken up, so that their traditional values lost all practical meaning.

INSTITUTIONAL DETERMINANTS OF POLITICAL BEHAVIOR

The characteristic political behavior of the various social groups in Hungary under Communism was decisively influenced, furthermore, by factors other than cultural background and traditional political orientation; namely, by factors related to the institutional environment that the Communists created for these groups. As in all Communist countries, the Party's control organs injected themselves into all the institutional settings that made up the fabric of Hungarian society: family, church, school, office, plant, the urban and rural market economy, the machinery of police and law enforcement, and so on. The Communists abolished some institutions altogether, notably the free market economy, and created some new ones such as the ruling party itself, the planned economy, and the collective farm. The surviving institutional settings were mostly thoroughly refashioned and placed under Party control or surveillance. The entire "mass" was controlled by the Party's representative organs in the institutions with which individual Hungarians were in permanent or intermittent contact. The manner and degree of control, however, differed considerably from one institutional setting to another, and it was these differences, above all, that accounted for the diversity in political behavior.

All the forms of political behavior observed in the mass had one thing in common: *spontaneous* compliance with the state's political directives was the exception rather than the rule. The individual citizen's "patriotic" identification with the Communist state did not go much beyond rooting for the Hungarian national team in international athletic competitions. Apart from this, "patriotism"—defined as identification, not with the timeless "fatherland," but with the existing state—was found, by and large, only in the elite. In the mass, conformity with the state's directives had to be elicited mostly by pressure, threats, and coercion.

Of particular relevance to the degree of control exercised by the state over any one individual was the institutional environment in which that person earned his living (plant, farm, laboratory, administrative office, and so on), as well as his hierarchical position within that setting. It is an optical illusion to believe that a totalitarian system relies mainly on police terror and thought control in its efforts to exact obedience from the mass. These features of totalitarianism are the most salient, the most visible from afar; they startle the imagination because they represent the sharpest contrast with normal life under democratic conditions. The person who lives under a Communist system, however, while very much aware of police terror and thought control, is subject to still other risks and pressures. In regulating his own behavior he can never forget the overwhelming fact that his livelihood is at the mercy of the various control organs of the state, particularly if he is just an ordinary member of the rank-and-file, not protected by the possession of unique skills or by social prestige. Purely economic threats such as dismissal, loss of employment possibilities, demotion, or reduction of income face the individual along with the harsher threat of terroristic measures (arrest, bodily harm, forced labor, loss of life). It is on the combination of these two types of threat that the Communist state relies to make everybody obey its directives. Certain coercive and deterrent effects are more easily achieved by economic sanctions than by terroristic threats alone. The latter are the more fearsome, but the former are less easy to evade and have far wider applicability. No management, for instance, can hand over to the police everybody who grumbles or whose work performance is slack, but it can quite easily fine all such persons.

Political Control and Institutional Environment

It is a distinctive feature of all totalitarian regimes that they insist upon regulating the political attitudes and behavior of their citizens according to a single pattern. Those citizens who identify themselves with the regime accept this regulation voluntarily; with the others, the state resorts to suggestion, intimidation, and direct coercion. When identification is very incomplete or nonexistent, such measures become the only means of shaping behavior. They can be carried to the greatest lengths in the institutional settings of the plant or administrative office, especially among the lower personnel. These settings lend themselves particularly well to what may be called "disciplinary control," that is to say, the constant surveillance over each low-status employee, combined with the threat of inescapable penalties in case of noncompliance with orders. In this manner, the Communist state, which has proprietary control over the entire urban economy, uses its disciplinary authority as employer to exact conformity of political behavior from lower office employees and industrial workers.

The disciplinary control of clerical personnel and industrial labor in Hungary meant the creation, in every office and plant, of an atmosphere of constant fear, a fear not only of terroristic measures but, above all, of economic sanctions. Wages being very low, even a small financial loss meant great hardship, not to speak of the effects of any permanent reduction of one's income or the loss of one's job. The disciplinary authorities could also make a person's life miserable by assigning him to disagreeable tasks or harassing him in other ways. The ordinary worker or clerical employee was defenseless in the face of all these threats. He had to obey the authorities, not only by fulfilling all work tasks, but also by avoiding the slightest departure from political conformity.

It should be noted that, in Hungary, the total disciplinary control of low-status "mass" elements by the agents of the elite affected outward behavior only, with little positive effect upon attitudes. Outward pressure did not produce inner loyalty. In the past, harsh and punitive authorities have indeed often succeeded in transforming the thinking of their subjects to the point of eliciting loyal attitudes, but this has been possible only where the fear of punishment was supplemented by the expectation of psychic gains. In Soviet Russia, such positive incentives seem to play a substantial role. For low-status Hungarian mass elements, however, conformist behavior hardly involved significant psychic rewards such as increased self-respect. Mostly, it meant escape from penalties. Skilled industrial workers were traditionally predisposed to feel pride in jobs well done, but even this was frequently rendered impossible by managerial bungling and directives conflicting with sound technological principles. As to the psychic rewards of self-respect gained from altruistic behavior, the feeling of serving the common good and being approved by the Party, they seem to have been nonexistent. In the beginning, rallying to the Communist Party and fulfilling its demands could confer such psychic advantages upon ordinary workers. After the Party assumed exclusive power, however, the regime's policies became totally divorced, in the eyes of the labor force, from any "collective interest," whether of class or of nation. Hence, the workers maintained a wholly negative inner attitude toward the regime, while their public behavior was conformist. The only departures from conformist behavior were clandestine acts such as stealing.

Nevertheless, the institutional setting of the plant left intact the feeling of cohesion and latent power among the industrial workers. They preserved their group identity, and the Communist state, while subjecting them to disciplinary control, also encouraged them to cultivate their class consciousness. This, apparently, was not the case with the clerical employees, who were maximally insecure and dependent without being able to claim the sacred group name of "proletariat." The lower office employees, therefore, were more thoroughly demoralized than the industrial workers; they apparently remained demoralized even after the outbreak of revolution.[1]

"COLLEGIAL" CONTROL

Institutional settings other than those of the plant and the administrative office, or a higher hierarchical position within these settings, tended to offer a measure of protection from complete control of the mass by the elite. Party organs, for example, could exercise relatively little control in such settings as the doctor's office, the scientific laboratory, and the research institute. Here, control was in the hands of experts with independent authority to whom the Party representatives had to defer, particularly if the experts' field was of great practical importance. The interview material reveals that doctors were generally considered the freest group in Hungary; indeed, it was commonly believed they could speak their minds with impunity. Also, experts' jobs often provided considerable protection for people who would otherwise have been regarded as "socially undesirable."

It was, however, not only professional experts with rare or unique qualifications who escaped the full rigors of disciplinary control. In the bureaucratic setting, too, the disciplinary control of middle and higher personnel runs counter to institutional traditions and is difficult to maintain in the long run. The traditional form of control here is the "collegial" one of a college or university: supervisors and subordinates have similar social standing, compliance with orders is supposed to be voluntary, and the relationship between different hierarchical levels is understood to be essentially one of solidarity rather than antagonism and coercion. In fact, bureaucratic operations cannot be conducted without delegation of authority; this requires the collegial form of control, just as does the management of operations involving high professional skill.

When the Communists took over the existing apparatus of

public and private bureaucracy and added to it a vast new one of their own, they fundamentally altered the bureaucratic institutional environment in order to impose upon it the Party's domination. The essential features of that environment—security of tenure, regulated advancement, admission contingent on the fulfillment of educational requirements—were abolished. Communists were advanced into all leading positions, with disregard for traditional schedules of advancement; many incumbents were eliminated because of their social background or past political affiliations; the remaining personnel were terrorized by the dominant Party apparatus. Collegial controls of the traditional, easy-going kind were replaced by disciplinary surveillance. The result was the destruction of the collective power of the old bureaucracies and of their *esprit de corps*. The dominant position of the Party apparatus rendered the non-Party elements dependent and insecure, subject to constant pressure. Moreover, the Communist power-holders themselves could not feel secure, because of the atmosphere of suspicion within the Party.

In spite of all this, however, traces of the old style of conducting bureaucratic operations re-emerged in many administrations. There had to be some delegation of authority, and the Communist top administrators were often too dependent on their staffs to maintain disciplinary rule. As a result, it frequently became possible for bureaucratic personnel, as it did for technical experts and professionals, to form small groups in which independent and critical attitudes and opinions were cultivated. This independence of thinking could not, of course, be translated into independent action; the bureaucracy was too dependent to resist official policies, although it was sometimes possible to apply the traditional bureaucratic strategy of stalling on the execution of orders on the grounds that they conflicted with standing rules and regulations.

The Communists' dominance could best be maintained in those administrative or professional bodies in which the top policy-makers were fanatical Communists, or ruthless careerists, who combined energy with professional competence. Wherever this condition prevailed, the non-Party intellectual or official was defenseless and terrorized. Another hazard was prosecution for sabotage whenever a serious mishap occurred in the course of operations (deaths of patients in hospitals, breakdown of machinery in plants, and so on). Such cases apart, however, the bureaucratic setting tended to allow a small leeway for critical independence and self-assertion.

THE SCHOOL ENVIRONMENT

The Communists' penetration into the institutional setting of the school seems to have been uneven. The setting as such did, of course, lend itself to close disciplinary surveillance of the pupils. (In this respect, the school environment resembles that of the industrial plant.) But this did not automatically ensure the Party's dominance, because institutional authority in the school rests with the teachers, and the Party was not in a position to fill all teaching posts with Communists. Nor was the school environment particularly well suited to the disciplinary supervision of teachers by administrative authorities. The Communists sought to solve this problem by entrusting the task of supervising the political behavior of teachers to Communist pupils, thus reversing the traditional authority relationship within the institutional setting of the school. This device gave the Communists an added measure of control, but it did not ensure complete control. (A pupil, after all, can report on a teacher and intimidate him, but he still cannot order him around.) Also, there were wide variations in the number of Party agents available among pupils and within the faculty, and the Party's measure of control, therefore, differed from one school to another. In some, Communist teachers and pupils maintained an atmosphere of terror; in others, the pupils put their Communist teachers on the defensive.

At the universities, Communist control seems to have been

more nearly complete than in the lower schools. If a professor did not see eye to eye with the Party, his authority as an expert gave him some protection. The students, however, could not escape the tyranny of the "cadre sheets." They knew that the Party's agents in the faculty and the student body were watching them and that any lapse from the prescribed behavior would be entered on their "cadre" file, a personal record on which their future careers depended. Total control over future jobs was the factor that enabled the Party to keep the students under its thumb by wielding the threat of undesirable assignments. Here, again, the threat that controlled behavior was economic rather than terroristic in nature. Even so, the students were not quite so helpless as were factory and office workers. They were accumulating rare and irreplaceable skills. Indeed, the state had made a considerable investment in each student by the time he reached an advanced stage in his studies, and the authorities could not crush the student's career without losing that investment. Students of proletarian origin were in a particularly strong position; for the regime deemed it essential to promote as many of them as possible to leading positions. As we noted earlier, the proletarian students were aware of this strategic advantage and made use of it.

Although the Party's control over the political behavior of the intelligentsia was less complete than its control over working-class behavior, the intelligentsia's inner attitudes were less uniformly and intensely hostile than those of the workers. In a good many cases, pressure upon intellectuals influenced not only outward behavior but also inner attitudes. The conforming intellectual achieved more than freedom from penalties; he could hope for considerable material advantages as well as for psychic gains. A position of prestige and power added to his self-esteem, and its attainment encouraged rationalizations in terms of the "common good." At any rate, the institutional setting in which the intellectuals lived was not conducive to a total contrast between outward behavior and inner attitude, to conforming under duress while inwardly maintaining unqualified hostility toward the regime. *Some* of the hostility they felt could be expressed; *some* of the conformity they showed was due to more than coercion.

THE RURAL SECTOR

Before World War I, the prevalence of large land holdings was a characteristic feature of the Hungarian agrarian economy; about 44 per cent of the land belonged to large owners with holdings of 115 hectares and over. In 1920, a limited land reform was carried out, in which about 415,000 hectares of land were distributed among 390,000 landless or land-poor peasants. This reform, however, was not sufficient to satisfy the land hunger of the peasants. It affected only 6 per cent of the total arable land, and it still left about 41 per cent of the land in the hands of large owners. In the thirties, 787,000 peasants had no land of their own; they lived on large estates as sharecropper tenants or hired workers. Another 552,000 peasants had less than one "hold" (0.576 hectare) of land, that is, less than was needed for subsistence farming; they had to do seasonal work on large estates to supplement their incomes. Together, the landless and land-poor made up more than half of the agricultural work force.[2]

Between the two wars, the land-hungry peasants had been insistent in demanding a more radical agricultural reform, but the political influence of the big landholding interests was overwhelming, and very little progress was made. However, defeat in World War II, and the entry of the Soviet troops into Hungary, completely changed the internal balance of political power: the old ruling groups became defenseless, and the big landed estates were doomed. A number of peasant leaders had long been waiting for such a turn of events and had prepared land-reform projects to be put into effect when the time was ripe. The Communists, however, did not allow the reform to be carried out under the auspices of the indigenous agrarian parties. The provisional government instituted a sweeping land reform on March 15, 1945, before the last German troops were driven from Hungarian soil; the decree was signed by Minister of Agriculture Imre Nagy, one of the few Communist members of the government. It was extremely important to the Communists that the land reform should be enacted speedily, that it should be radical in scope, and that the main credit for it should go to the Party.

There was nothing Marxian about the reform itself. It broke up all land holdings of over 100 "holds" (57.6 hectares) and distributed a large part of the land fund thus secured among landless and land-poor peasants. Of the 3.2 million hectares confiscated, 1.9 million were distributed among 642,000 families, the rest being declared state property. Thus, the main effect of the reform was that it created a large number of new independent peasant holdings and made others, formerly too small to support a family, economically self-sustaining.

This strengthening of the independent peasant economy was completely at variance with the agricultural policies of Soviet Russia, whose keynote was collectivization. Yet the Hungarian Communist Party, in championing diffuse private property in agriculture, had good political reasons for adopting this policy, since there was no other way to acquire a mass following. After all, Lenin had also proclaimed the "alliance between the working peasantry and the proletariat" as a necessary element in the success of socialist revolution, and had encouraged the peasants to seize the land, although to him as a Marxist, individual landholding could only be an interim expedient. To the Hungarian Communists, too, the land-hungry peasants appeared indispensable as auxiliaries during the difficult period of seizing and consolidating state power; later, the time would come when individual ownership could and would be abolished in the agricultural as it had been in the industrial sector of the economy. During the early stages of their rise to total power, at any rate, the Communists disclaimed any intention of abolishing the system of individual landholding, and denounced as base slanderers all those who suggested that once the Communists had their way, they would seek to introduce the kolkhoz system in Hungary.

This, however, was precisely what happened after the establishment of the Communist one-party state, when a drive was begun to consolidate the hundreds of thousands of peasant holdings. The process was to be accomplished by stages. Three distinct types of "productive cooperatives" were developed: members in the two lower types were allowed to retain some title to the land and cattle contributed by them; members in the highest type were required to pool land, livestock, and inventory almost completely. It was, of course, this highest type that the regime was most anxious to encourage. After the collectivization campaign got under way, the Hungarian peasants lived in one or another of three institutional settings: the state farm, the "productive cooperative" or kolkhoz, and the small holding, the first two being "socialized," and the third private. Of the three kinds of environment, the third alone was congenial to them, but the regime did everything in its power to drive the small peasant out of business. On the state farms and kolkhozes, there was no room for independent decisions by the peasants themselves; all work was regulated from distant higher offices. Since spontaneous cooperation could not develop in these circumstances, the regime increasingly tried to impose a tight disciplinary control upon the agricultural population. Work was to be performed in "brigades" and "links," organized on the pattern of military units and factory teams. The peasants found this utterly humiliating.

Disciplinary control, however, was not only resented by the peasants; it also was impossible to impose in the rural setting with anything like the completeness permitted by the office or plant environment. Agricultural work is very different from the tending of machinery in a shop. It does not consist of standardized, identical operations. What is more, the workers are not confined in a small place where they can be supervised, and the result of most of their operations can be seen and judged only after considerable time. Hence, it is practically impossible to force the individual by disciplinary pressure to perform according to specifications. Everything depends on how much or how little effort he himself chooses to expend.

Peasants will make extraordinary efforts if their hearts are in it; that is, if they are working for themselves and hope to get a fair return. On kolkhoz land, however, this was not the case, and Communist disciplinary control was not strong enough to prevent them from deliberately restricting their output.

Communist control organs never entered the institutional setting of independent farming; the Communists' aim was not to control but to destroy the institution. Hence they multiplied both terroristic and economic penalties for peasants who insisted upon independence, but their success with this method was slow and incomplete. The peasants were the only class in a position to put up a real fight against being uprooted and enslaved by the Communists. The middle class could be expropriated by a stroke of the pen; the bureaucracy could be purged and deprived of its *esprit de corps* and security of position as soon as the Party seized exclusive control of the government; the workers could be reduced to impotence by the Party's taking over their organizations and subjecting them to disciplinary control. In all urban institutional settings, the Communists' drive for domination was irresistible; for their political power enabled them to gain control over everybody's livelihood. In the rural environments, however, neither organizational maneuvers nor administrative decisions were sufficient to forestall or break individual resistance. The authorities actually had to face the peasant in a contest of wills. Overwhelming power was on the Party's side, but this was not enough to compel the peasants to maximum productive effort within the institutional setting the Communists had designed for them. Control over the level of output largely remained with the peasants themselves, and this fact turned out to be an effective limitation upon the Communist state's potentialities for coercion.

8

PATTERNS OF
REVOLUTIONARY
BEHAVIOR

THE ELITE

For months before the revolt, the intra-Party opposition had been demanding the rehabilitation of Nagy and the reorganization of the government under his leadership; otherwise, the opponents of the Old Guard warned, there would be an explosion. The opposition, however, had no thought of forcing the hand of those in power. To all Party men, however critical of the regime, a change in leadership not decided upon by the appropriate Party authorities was unthinkable. Events, however, outran the sluggish tempo of intra-Party developments. The explosion came, but the old leadership was still in place, and no preparations had been made for reshuffling the top positions in the Party.

Nagy himself was out of town when the students began preparing their mass demonstration. It was the wine harvest season, and he had gone to a small country place he owned in the wine district of western Hungary. There, on the evening of October 22, Nagy was guest of honor at a wine harvest festival, while the Budapest students were holding meetings and formulating revolutionary demands, including the one that called for a new government under his leadership. Nagy learned about this from the radio on the 23rd, and decided to return to Budapest.[1] Nothing, however, was further from his thoughts than taking advantage of this irregular popular movement in his favor in order to crush his old Party antagonists and impose himself as leader. According to Meray, who himself was an active member of the intra-Party opposition and conversant with Nagy's political attitudes at that time, some of the students' demands, notably those directed against Soviet domination, were far too radical for Nagy to swallow.[2] Moreover, Nagy would not have considered taking any political initiative outside Party channels.

The only Party people imaginative and undisciplined enough to take direct action to bring about a last-minute change of government were the journalists of the Party newspaper *Szabad Nép*. After an impromptu meeting at the newspaper's offices, they sent a delegation to the Central Committee, urging the leadership to bow to the will of the people. Gerö, who received the delegation, waved the suggestion aside.[3]

During the afternoon of the 23rd, when the city was already in an uproar, Nagy stayed at home. With great difficulty, some of his supporters, including the novelist Tamás Aczél, persuaded him to go to the parliament building, in front of which a huge crowd was clamoring to hear him. Nagy, having no instructions from the Party authorities, at first refused to talk to the crowd. When, finally, he appeared on the balcony and spoke a few words, it was a near disaster. He began with the word "Comrades" and was roundly booed. In his short address, he stressed the need to proceed within the framework of "constitutional order and discipline." The crowd then began to disperse; many went to the radio building, where fighting broke out soon afterward.[4]

During the night, the Central Committee finally decided to appoint Nagy Premier. Installed in power, however, Nagy did not, at first, act like a revolutionary leader. His primary endeavor upon taking office was to restore order and disarm the insurgents. His appeals to the fighters to lay down their arms were fruitless (understandably enough, since Soviet tanks were in action in the capital), and his initial popularity declined rapidly.[5]

The Communist intellectuals, who had been the most radical and outspoken critics of the regime before the revolution, were thoroughly frightened by its outbreak and did everything in their power to steer events into a peaceful course. Gyula Háy, for example, spoke as follows in a broadcast to young Hungarians on October 25:

> There must be a change-over to peaceful methods without the slightest delay, the armed struggle must stop immediately. Even peaceful demonstrations are not suitable at this time, because they can be misconstrued. There must now begin an implacable, uncompromising, democratic clash of thoughts and ideas in which the spokesmen of the new, the young in age and spirit, will gain a brilliant, universally resounding victory.[6]

According to Háy, Gerö's removal from power[7] guaranteed that all legitimate revolutionary aspirations would be satisfied under the new government.

The Communist writers' efforts to call a halt to violent action indicated no change in their fundamental attitudes. They did not give up their convictions, either then or later. Their determination "never again to tell lies" held good, after the crushing of the revolution, under the Kádár regime. Háy, Déry, and other leading Communist critics of the pre-revolutionary regime who stayed in Hungary never recanted; they went to prison rather than submit. Their behavior showed a remarkable consistency before, during, and after the revolution: they wanted to reform the regime, to rid it of its aberrations, but they had no idea of discarding Marxist socialism as the basis of political order and starting out along entirely new lines.

Nagy, too, was consistent; he thought he could save the situation in 1956 by reviving the New Course of 1953. Only gradually did he perceive that the dynamism of the revolution had rendered that stage hopelessly obsolete. When he did recognize this fact, he prepared himself to make a revolutionary break with the past. The formation of a government of national union, announced on October 27, represented the beginning of such a break; it was followed by more radical steps in the same direction, culminating in the attempted withdrawal from the Soviet bloc.[8] Nagy, however, did not choose this radical course spontaneously; he was forced into it by the uncontrollable, overwhelming upsurge of the masses' revolutionary *élan*.

THE MASS

The Social Background of the Combatants

The proportion of active fighters in the revolution varied from one social group to another. A survey conducted by the Audience Analysis Section of Radio Free Europe, Munich, gives the following breakdown of the proportion of active fighters within the various social categories: professionals, 14 per cent; white-collar, 2 per cent; industrial workers, 13 per cent; farmers and farmhands, 6 per cent; and others (including students), 20 per cent.[9]

This breakdown shows the highest incidence of active fighting in the last group, the youngest in age, who were not yet classifiable in any occupational category other than that of students. The urban occupational groups, except clerical workers, follow next. The peasantry shows a much lower percentage, and the office workers the lowest of all. (Of the total white-collar group, 82 per cent are shown as having been "inactive"; that is, as not even having participated in non-fighting activities.)

The peasantry had its own pattern of revolutionary activity. This class seems to have been in sympathy with the most aggressive revolutionary groups, the active fighters; it did not want a "reformed" Communism but was seeking something radically different. The peasants showed their sympathy by supplying the fighters with food. Their own activity, however, was concentrated largely upon dismantling the kolkhozes, their constant objective throughout the Communist era. Their behavior, somewhat like that of "elite" rebels, showed continuity rather than an abrupt change from submission to rebellion.

Some continuity also could be observed in the behavior of the intelligentsia: the members of this category reveled in proclaiming publicly what they had long been saying *sotto voce* in private. They devoted much energy to creating a democratic political machinery. There was a proliferation of newspapers and political parties[10] reflecting every shade of opinion. Interview material reveals that many of the fighters (students, in particular) felt this activity to be both excessive and premature; it deflected energies from the main task. The intelligentsia, however, were extremely active in every field of revolutionary endeavor, literary and organizational work as well as armed combat; the Radio Free Europe survey shows that the proportion of the "inactive" in this class was only 6 per cent, as compared to 61 to 82 per cent in the other classes.

The extremely low participation quota among office workers is striking: it suggests that this category remained demoralized even after the outbreak of revolution. The group as a whole was apparently unable to develop an organizational framework of its own, or to attach itself to the various councils in which the industrial workers, the intelligentsia, and the students ranged themselves.

Extreme combativeness manifested itself in the Hungarian Revolution primarily among three categories of people: street crowds who assembled in spontaneous fashion, the youngest age group, and industrial workers. Each group had its own characteristic style of revolutionary behavior.

The Street Crowds

In the crowds, tension built up gradually during the afternoon and evening of October 23. What attracted them to begin with was the sight of marching students; this was something entirely new and exhilarating. But at first the street crowds were mere onlookers, curious to see what would happen. As time went by, however, the people's mood gradually changed. When the crowds grew denser and showed no inclination to disperse, it dawned upon those in them that a historic moment was at hand. We find in the interviews such statements as: "We simply felt that it was impossible to leave without having done something decisive"; and "Something big was bound to happen." The crowds now sought outlets for this accumulated tension. The statue of Stalin offered itself as a target. Vast numbers converged upon the parliament building, clamoring for Imre Nagy, whom the street had designated premier, and upon the radio building, where they took up the students' demand that their manifesto be put on the air. When the police attacked, nobody thought of dispersing. The provocation drove the crowd to frenzy, and the possession of arms, obtained from sympathizers among the military, gave it a feeling of unlimited power. The crowd's ruling impulse was to destroy the symbols of Communist and Soviet domination and to get even with the terror and publicity apparatus of the regime. The offices of the Party newspaper (by then under the control of Communist dissidents) were wrecked; bonfires were built of Communist literature; the hated red star emblem was torn down everywhere. Above all, the crowd stormed the strongholds of the political police and overpowered the units manning them. There were many lynchings.

This phase of the revolution exhibited many of the well-

111

known features of mob violence: rage, a passionate desire for revenge, cruelty. Yet one of the classic symptoms of mass action, the breakdown of cultural restraints and inhibitions, was lacking. Mass aggression was extremely selective, pinpointed upon the political police.[11] There was no looting, no storming of shops, no general breakdown of discipline. The crowds did not even start an indiscriminate persecution of Communists. Even in small towns, where Party members were highly conspicuous, "decent" Communists were left unharmed. On the whole, destructive impulses were vented only upon the political police and the inanimate symbols of Communist rule.

The Young People

The revolution entered a new, fateful stage after the entry of Soviet occupation troops in the early morning of October 24. During this stage, the revolutionary struggle consisted mainly of street battles with Soviet tanks, and in these the youngest age group played the most conspicuous part. To a very considerable extent, the street battles were fought by the young: students, apprentices, and schoolchildren. A good many older people participated too, but it seems certain that the struggle would not have been sustained as long as it was if it had not been for the death-defying, desperate determination of the very young.

According to the above-mentioned survey of Radio Free Europe, 11 per cent of the population up to 20 years of age, and 19 per cent of those aged between 21 and 29, were active fighters in the revolution. Among those between 30 and 49 years old, however, only 5 per cent fought actively, and of those aged 50 years or more, 1 per cent.[12] The fall-off after 29 years of age is significant. How can this be explained? Whereas it is not surprising that people aged 50 and over showed little inclination to participate in street battles, men in their 30's are not too old to fight. On the other hand, those aged 32 or

112

more in 1956 were old enough to have seen military service in World War II. They had had experience with Soviet tanks and could estimate the odds against successful resistance. This, presumably, was the reason why they showed less inclination to fight than those who had not been in the war. A Hungarian war veteran whom I interviewed was very positive on this point. He said that ex-soldiers considered military resistance to the Russians hopeless; only boys too young to have seen service were ignorant enough to fight. This extreme formulation certainly overstates the case, but the general point seems valid.

The very young among the active fighters did not, in fact, base their action upon any sort of realistic weighing of odds. There was in their combativeness an element of psychic compulsion, as though they were caught in a somnambulistic trance. It did not matter whether they lived or died. Only one thing counted: getting weapons and using them as much and as long as possible.

How did such a pattern of behavior develop among children? Lack of suitable data makes it impossible to answer this question conclusively. On general grounds, however, it seems that decisive weight must be given to peer-group solidarity and imitation. When some children got weapons and went out to fight, this apparently started a teen-age epidemic: the others felt they could not remain behind. Not every child fought, of course; presumably, *all* parents did what they could to restrain their own children, and many succeeded. However, the Radio Free Europe figure of 11 per cent for active fighters in the age group up to 20 by no means gives the true measure of the scope of the teen-age epidemic in Budapest. For one thing, the sample is nationwide, but most of the active fighting took place in Budapest; for another, the age span includes the many children not yet in the teen-group who were immune to the epidemic or could be controlled by their parents.

Whereas children mostly fought in small gangs, the combat

activity of more mature young men, particularly students, showed a more organized pattern. The students had organizations of their own to begin with. Within these, various teams were formed for specific purposes (the printing and distribution of leaflets; liaison with the workers, the army, and the government; active fighting; and logistic support). Interviews with students indicate that they considered themselves the nerve center of the revolution. They found that they could easily establish contact with any group—workers and peasants as well as government officials, professionals, and army officers. They used this easy access to all strata in order to coordinate revolutionary policies and activities.

The Industrial Workers

It was the industrial workers whose revolutionary activity lasted longest and was the best organized. They were active in street battles in Budapest and elsewhere; but their weightiest contribution to the revolutionary struggle was the organization of workers' councils and, its principal outcome, the revolutionary general strike.

The first workers' council was set up at the Incandescent Lamp Factory in Budapest on October 24. From there, the movement spread rapidly; within three days, a network of councils covered the entire country.[13] The councils' activity was concentrated on national politics. For example, on October 26, one of the most articulate of the councils, that of the industrial region of Borsod County, north of Budapest, broadcast a manifesto of twenty-one points, which a delegation took to Budapest and submitted to Premier Nagy.[14]

The Borsod program contained a number of demands reflecting the social welfare aims of organized labor (better wages, workers' control of plants, decentralization of industry, and so on), but the significant thing about it was that it put the greatest emphasis not on social but on national grievances. It urged revision of the trade treaties with the Soviet Union, the exploitation of the Hungarian uranium deposits for the country's benefit, and, above all, the withdrawal of Soviet occupation troops by January 1, 1957, at the latest. To give effect to these demands, the Borsod workers proclaimed a general strike, to last until the occupation was lifted. In the sequel, the activity of all workers' councils was concentrated upon this basic point. Work stopped in all plants. The workers knew that the strike would bring great hardships, but they did not care; if existing conditions could not be altered radically, they felt, life was not worth living anyway. When the revolution seemed to be victorious, the councils made preparations to end the strike. But after the second Soviet intervention, they decided to keep it up, and the condition for resuming work remained the same: the withdrawal of the Soviet troops. The workers simply disregarded the verdict of military action, refusing to believe that their collective effort could be frustrated by it.

To my knowledge, this was the first time in history that the syndicalist myth of the revolutionary general strike, as set forth by Georges Sorel, actually became the basis of sustained political action by the entire industrial population of a country. It is safe to say that the Hungarian workers who organized the councils and conceived the idea of a general strike against the Russian occupation had never heard of Sorel and his theory of the "myth," but they acted in accordance with it. There was only this difference: Sorel thought that the proletariat would rise to sweep away a rotten, degenerate bourgeois order, but to his unwitting Hungarian disciples the antithesis between "bourgeoisie" and "proletariat" was of no immediate interest. The significant antithesis was between "Soviet" and "Hungarian," and the social and political order to be swept away was not a bourgeois but a Communist one, set up by the disciples of Lenin whom Sorel had greatly admired. The idea of workers' councils seems to have been inspired by the example of Yugoslavia, where a new type of "industrial self-government," based upon the creation of plant councils, had been introduced in 1950.[15] A council movement inspired by the same example arose in the autumn of 1956 in Poland, where the councils mobilized the industrial masses and created popular pressure strong enough to compel a relaxation of the dictatorship and some easing of Soviet control. In Poland, however, the councils never became supreme, because the Party apparatus was not smashed, but merely revamped under Gomulka's leadership. By contrast, the Hungarian councils were able to steer a radical revolutionary course. They insisted upon the total elimination of all Party influences from economic management as well as from national politics. The end of Soviet occupation was the underlying aim of all this, and the council movement became primarily a national liberation movement.

The workers' revolutionary behavior showed a sharp break in continuity. Outwardly quiet until the outbreak of street fighting in Budapest, the Hungarian industrial population instantly mobilized itself in a determined bid to wrest political power from the Party. This explosive transition from total discipline to total rebellion was characteristic of the "mass pattern" of the Hungarian Revolution, in contrast with the smooth, continuous nature of the "elite pattern." Not that the revolutionary behavior of the mass represented a completely new departure; the Hungarian Revolution consciously imitated historical models. The memories of 1848–49 (Kossuth's and Petöfi's revolution) were ever-present. In addition, the industrial workers in revolting against the Party were inspired by the Social Democratic traditions of the organized labor movement of Hungary. These traditions, suppressed under the Communist regime, suddenly came to the fore when the workers regained their freedom of action.

THE MOTIVATION OF THE FIGHTING

Analysis of Hungarian revolutionary behavior, both in the elite and in the mass, suggests this over-all conclusion: combative impulses resulted, generally speaking, from a combination of two factors, namely, bitterness and frustration on the one hand, and a feeling of strength on the other. Hungarian revolutionary behavior was not a sudden desperate reaction to intolerable pressure and deprivation. It was, rather, a delayed reaction to all the negative experiences of the past, a reaction released when elements of weakness appeared in the image of the regime, and elements of strength bulked larger in one's own self-image.

Thus, it was the "thaw" originating in Soviet Russia, a loosening in the fabric of dictatorship, that sparked active opposition in the disaffected part of the elite. Similarly, the peasants responded to the regime's retreat in the summer of 1953 by active revolt. The mass revolt in Budapest broke out when the crowds saw that the students could demonstrate with impunity, and when numbers and excitement gave them a feeling of strength. Finally, it was the collapse of the Communist power structure that gave the signal for nationwide revolt.

A related point is that propensity for rebellious action was not directly proportional to the psychic distance separating the individual from the regime. Those who had the amplest grounds for complaint were not the most prone to rebel. People who had lost everything tended to be demoralized and passive, whereas revolutionary activity originated with groups who were partly privileged and partly frustrated.[16] The writers, who were the first to rebel, had a highly privileged social and economic position, but suffered acutely from the loss of personal integrity and professional satisfaction; the students who followed suit were nurtured by the regime and could expect to rise into relatively high social brackets, but they resented regimentation and forced indoctrination. Both groups inevitably accepted certain features of the regime to which they owed their status. Even such ideological closeness to the regime, however, did not preclude radical political opposition to it. This was not surprising: although strong political antago-

117

nism to a system may have its origin in total rejection of the system's principles, it may also spring from dissatisfaction with the way in which the principles, accepted as such, are being carried out. In fact, disappointed expectations are particularly likely to result in violent hatred. One may learn to live with an enemy from whom one never expected anything but evil, but it is impossible not to feel aggressive impulses toward a treacherous friend.

The gulf between "promises" and "reality" is a recurrent motif in the interviews with Hungarians; numerous respondents described this contrast as the most difficult thing to endure. It was most glaring for the industrial workers, who had been promised not only a good life in general, but a dominant position in the state, and who in actual fact were subjected to a particularly relentless form of regimentation and harassment. As we have seen, the disciplinary control that the Communist economic authorities exercised over the workers was strong enough to inhibit open opposition. At the same time, the workers felt that they had claims upon the state which were theirs by right; that is, by virtue of basic principles proclaimed by the Communists themselves. They were prepared to present these claims as soon as disciplinary controls were shaken off. If their material position was weak and dependent, their moral position vis-à-vis the apparatus always remained strong; for, given the freedom to talk and act, they could attack the regime in the name of principles that the Communist rulers themselves had to recognize as unassailable. This was an important strategic factor in the revolution. It contributed to the breakup of the Communist elite, some sections of which were intensely aware of the weakness of their moral position. It also facilitated the coordination of revolutionary forces, since it gave the opposition a noncontroversial platform.

9

STABILITY

AND

INSTABILITY

THE NEW COURSE AND ITS EFFECTS

The outbreak of the Hungarian Revolution of October 1956 marked the climax of a political crisis that had been going on for more than three years. The stability of the Hungarian Communist regime received its first severe jolt in the summer of 1953 with the announcement of the New Course. The immediate effect was division in the Party leadership; this became progressively aggravated until the whole authority structure of the regime was hollowed out. In the end, the regime was no longer able to withstand the onslaught of the masses.

Now, the New Course of 1953 was not an isolated Hungarian phenomenon. An analogous reorientation of basic policies took place in all satellite countries about the same time. After Stalin's death, the entire satellite area was engulfed in a severe economic crisis, brought about by forced industrialization and collectivization. Stalin's successors in Moscow realized that a retreat from the unrealistic, overambitious goals of the earlier program was imperative. They called for a relaxation of the ruthless economic drives that had been initiated, and at the same time they also moved to do away with the terroristic methods that had caused ravages in the Party's ranks in the great purges of the preceding period.

119

This drastic reorientation involved a potential threat to the stability of the satellite regimes. In acknowledging the failure of these basic policies every Communist leadership was discredited, and exposed to possible challenges either from an internal Party opposition or from the people at large. At the same time, the weakening of the terror apparatus made it problematic how effectively the leaders could deal with such challenges. As events have shown, some of the satellite regimes—those of Rumania, Bulgaria, and Albania—were able to weather the reorientation crisis of 1953 without major disturbances or threats to their stability. The others, however, were not. Not only in Hungary, but also in Czechoslovakia, East Germany, and Poland, acute crisis symptoms developed in the wake of the New Course.

The evolution of the crisis touched off by the New Course followed different patterns in the four countries. To begin with, the New Course itself was launched at different times and in different ways in the several satellites. In East Germany and Hungary, the announcement of the New Course came early (in June–July 1953) and took the most dramatic form possible, with great emphasis on past mistakes and on the magnitude of the changes to be brought about. In the other satellite countries, the change-over to the New Course was announced later (in August–September 1953) and with much less fanfare.

The crisis symptoms that followed were also different. There were large-scale industrial disorders in Czechoslovakia and East Germany in June, at the very beginning of the New Course period, and things settled down to normal thereafter. In Poland and Hungary, on the other hand, the introduction of the New Course did not touch off acute disturbances (apart from the wave of agrarian riots in Hungary, which hardly touched the nerve center of political life); it did, however, result in a chronic crisis within the leadership, which progressively unbalanced the situation over the years. Severe mass disorders broke out in these two countries only in 1956, three years after the original stimulus given by the New Course. For this renewed disturbance, the initial impulse again came from Moscow. It was the Twentieth Congress of the CPSU, and Khrushchev's speech in particular, that gave the leadership crisis in Poland and Hungary a new critical turn; whereas the effects produced by the Congress in the other satellite countries were far less drastic.

How can these different patterns of development be explained? The question has general importance, for it takes us to the very heart of the problem of political stability in the totalitarian state. To be sure, no exhaustive answer can be attempted at this time; as long as the governmental and Party archives of the satellite area and of Moscow remain closed, many crucial matters have to be left to speculation. We may, however, hope to draw some general conclusions from a comparison of events of public record. To this end, we shall briefly review the revolutionary and near-revolutionary events and processes of the post-Stalin period in Czechoslovakia, East Germany, and Poland. These will be compared with Hungarian developments, a comparison which, it is hoped, will suggest a number of factors relevant to the political stability or instability of Communist regimes.

Our analysis will focus upon the above-mentioned four satellite countries, in which the New Course produced the most serious effects, whether of acute trouble or chronic instability. Not that these effects can be understood without reference to outside factors. For any relaxation or tightening of the policy line of a satellite government, the decisive impulse always came from Moscow, and the center's decisions always reflected the status of the various leaders and coteries contending for power in the Kremlin. To some extent, the varying policies adopted by the Soviet Union and imposed upon the satellites also represented more or less unavoidable responses to economic facts (such as inflationary pressures) that affected all the satellite countries, and sometimes the Soviet Union itself as well. Yet it is possible to treat the satellites as representing a special category, for which the New Course, for example, meant something different from what it did for the Soviet Union. Industrialization and collectivization (the chief economic issues involved in the New Course) belonged to different historical periods in the two areas: in the Soviet Union, they were essentially solved before World War II; in the satellites, they represented a recent venture, which in 1952–53 created acute crisis symptoms that had no parallel in the Soviet setting. The same applies to the great intra-Party purges: in Russia, in the fifties, these were definitely a thing of the past, whereas in the satellites their memory was still fresh. The New Course, then, raised special problems in the satellite countries, requiring treatment in local terms.

We shall observe how different local conditions led to different responses in the Communist leadership and the mass from one country to another. It is not implied, however, that independent local initiative was mainly responsible for these variations. Little room was left for such initiative, because, first, the Moscow center maintained constant, tight control over satellite governmental decisions and, second, every local Communist Party was itself attuned to Moscow and would initiate only such policies as could be expected to meet with the Soviet leaders' approval. Even the intra-Party opposition groups that eventually developed formidable strength in Poland and Hungary were more anti–Old Guard in their local setting than they were anti-Soviet. They, too, hoped to win Moscow's approval in the end, even though they were determined to show some defiance, necessary in view of the bitter mood of the masses. Both in 1953 and in 1956, reforming or opposition elements in satellite Communist Parties were able to claim orthodoxy and to invoke Moscow's authority in support of their programs.

Communists in the satellite countries were not ready to cut adrift from the Soviet Union, although they sometimes indulged in covert or even overt resistance to the center's wishes (the conservatives trying to inhibit impetuous reforms and the reformers seeking to resist regressive policies).

Only the unrehearsed, spontaneous insurrectional moves of the masses were of wholly indigenous inspiration. Yet the masses' behavior, too, reflected the changing attitudes and postures of the Communist power-holders. The weakening of pressure from above was a necessary factor in all large-scale outbreaks of mass violence. In some cases, as we shall see, the pattern was more complex—the weakening of pressure in general coincided with fresh economic impositions which directly provoked the masses. This contradictory dual pattern was particularly conspicuous in the Czech and East German disturbances that broke out at the beginning of the post-Stalin era.

THE PLZEN UPRISING

The first major upheaval in the Communist bloc following Stalin's death occurred in Czechoslovakia, a country whose standard of living was relatively high as compared to the other satellites. As elsewhere in the bloc, the economic situation in the spring of 1953 was extremely strained; agricultural production had decreased catastrophically because of the peasants' resistance to collectivization, food rations could not be met, and there were inflationary price increases. The government, however, at first tried to cope with the situation without reorienting its basic policies and without admitting any mistakes. It decided, instead, to put an end to the inflationary crisis by revaluing the currency.

Under the monetary decree issued on May 30, 1953, bank notes as well as bank deposits were exchanged at progressive rates varying between 5:1 and 50:1, with people possessing up to 300 crowns in cash and up to 5,000 crowns in deposits receiving the most favorable rate. Nominal prices were reduced to one-fifth. The measure was aimed, in the first place, at independent farmers and small businessmen who had accumulated large amounts of cash during the preceding inflationary period. With the purchasing power of this group curtailed, the government hoped, excess demand for consumer goods would be siphoned off and the price level would be stabilized. At the same time, the regime claimed that the reform would hit only exploiters and capitalists; the workers' material interests would not be affected.

In actual fact, however, the working class was hit very hard. For one thing, many workers had savings, which were practically wiped out by the reform; for another, the reform reduced real earnings for many, especially the lowest paid, because food prices remained out of line with the adjusted incomes. After the announcement of the currency reform, feeling ran high in the Czech factory towns, especially among the workers' wives, who complained bitterly about the diminished purchasing power of their husband's earnings. On June 1, extremely violent, politically tinged riots broke out in Plzen; there was also rioting, and possibly a general strike, in the Moravská Ostrava coal-mining area between May 30 and June 4.[1]

At Plzen, on June 1, five thousand workers reportedly staged a protest march against the currency reform. They went to the City Hall, where the mayor addressed the crowd but was not able to pacify it. The demonstrators then broke into the building and tore down pictures of Stalin and Gottwald. There were demands for free elections; the names of Masaryk, Benes, and Eisenhower were cheered. A small military unit sent to the scene refused to fire on the demonstrators. Finally, the riot was quelled by border guards and police troops dispatched from Prague.

The main features of the Czechoslovak incidents of June 1953 may be summarized as follows:

(1) The outbreaks were touched off by an acute provoca-

tion: a governmental decree tampering with the people's purchasing power.

(2) Violent protest was voiced by the industrial workers only. The other groups whose material interests were affected by the currency reform remained passive.

(3) No "elite pattern" was discernible in the insurrection. It was purely a mass movement, unrehearsed and spontaneous. No division was apparent in the Party leadership. In fact, the Party was still going through the purge stage; the brother of Rudolf Slansky (the Party Secretary liquidated during the previous year) had been sentenced as an imperialist spy, together with three associates, just a few days before the riots broke out.

(4) Although the immediate motive for the workers' protest movement was a financial one, the movement itself went far beyond mere demands for redress. The workers were attacking the regime as such.

(5) Order was restored without great difficulty by special police troops, after the conscript army refused to open fire.

The Plzen uprising was unique in one respect: unlike the disturbances that occurred later in other parts of the satellite area, it was not preceded by an explicit denunciation of past policies by the Communist authorities themselves. It thus falls outside the general pattern of instability associated with the New Course, a pattern in which division within the Communist elite is essential. In a wider sense, however, Plzen was very much part of the post-Stalin crisis of the Soviet bloc. The currency decree itself was an implicit avowal of failure: it demonstrated that the regime could not make ends meet and was forced to renege on some of its financial obligations to the people. This was a manifestation of weakness to which the industrial masses responded by rebellion.

THE EAST GERMAN REVOLT

After Stalin's death, the East German economy was in desperate straits as a result of forced industrialization and agricultural collectivization. Many independent farmers, harassed by exorbitant, punitive taxes and delivery quotas, restricted production or abandoned their farmsteads and fled to the West; owners of small independent businesses and workshops, whose output was an essential component of the East German economy, did likewise. In fact, the East German middle strata, threatened in their economic existence by Communist policies, had an opportunity open to them that their opposite numbers in other satellite areas did not have: they could flee their tormentors and start afresh in West Germany.[2] The regime, angered by this form of passive resistance, responded with increased terror against the middle strata. In the spring of 1953, decrees were issued raising agricultural delivery quotas and ordering the forcible collection of delinquent taxes. In April, the ration cards of all "class-alien" elements (house owners, artisans, businessmen, industrialists, and some professional people) of the Soviet zone and Berlin's eastern sector, as well as those of East Berliners employed in West Berlin, were stopped. These measures were designed to crush the East German "bourgeoisie" and to confiscate whatever economic substance was left to them so as to make sure that the flight of people to the West could no longer constitute a drain on the Soviet zone's capital assets.

At the same time, the screws were put on to exact more production from the industrial workers. In the spring of 1953, the Communist labor organizations started a systematic drive to induce the workers to raise their output quotas. This drive was unsuccessful; the workers were incensed about the steady deterioration of their standard of living owing to inflationary price increases and felt that output norms were, if anything, already too high. The Communists, however, persevered. Meeting on May 13–14, the Party's Central Committee adopted a resolution calling for the immediate revision of all work norms. On May 28, the Council of Ministers of the "German Democratic Republic" ordered all output norms to be raised by at least 10 per cent. This was to be achieved by June 30, 1953, and was to be followed by a systematic overhauling of the entire norm system that would ensure even greater increases.[3]

The various repressive measures of the spring of 1953 had a shattering effect upon the population. The exodus to West Germany assumed enormous proportions. (About 185,000 persons fled during the first five months of 1953, as compared to about 150,000 during the whole year 1952.) In the plants, there were heated discussions on the norm increases; many workers remonstrated openly and vehemently.[4]

As the situation was thus rapidly deteriorating, the East German government, prodded by Moscow, was preparing concessions to the middle strata, calculated to stop the westward flight of people and capital. On April 15, Malenkov advised the East German regime to adopt a NEP-like "New Course," mitigating the rigors of forced collectivization, in order to end the acute economic crisis; nothing else could bring relief, since the Soviet Union was not in a position to provide financial help.[5] During the following weeks, the Soviet government increased its pressure upon its East German puppets. On April 22, Semyonov, the political adviser of the Soviet Control Commission (a man known for his moderate and conciliatory attitude), was recalled to Moscow and made Deputy Foreign Minister. On May 28, the Soviet Control Commission itself was dissolved, and Semyonov reappeared in East Berlin, this time as Soviet High Commissioner. He seems to have carried stringent instructions for swift and drastic action. On June 9, he called a meeting of the Politburo of the SED (the East German Communist Party), which adopted a resolution that amounted to a total reversal of the regime's political line.[6]

The resolution of the Politburo stated that the SED and the government had committed a series of grave errors that called for correction. It condemned the stopping of the food cards, the raising of agricultural delivery quotas, the new stringent taxation measures. It criticized the Party and the government for neglecting the interests of the independent businessmen, small entrepreneurs, farmers, and professionals and called for immediate remedies. The Party and the government were instructed to take action to improve the standard of living of all strata of the population and to strengthen legal safeguards of personal rights.

The resolution enumerated a long list of specific measures by which to correct old and recent abuses. For example, food cards were to be restored forthwith to people who had been deprived of them, and delinquent taxes were to be remitted. Dispossessed small merchants and artisans were to be encouraged to reopen their businesses; confiscated land was to be given back to all farmers who returned from West Germany; delivery quotas were to be reduced. There was also to be an amnesty for people who had been convicted of offenses against "national property" (that is, plant thefts).[7]

This package resolution, published on June 11, caused an enormous sensation. The stern judgment pronounced on the Party and the government struck a mortal blow to the regime's authority. There was a feeling of expectancy. The industrial workers were particularly excited; for the package resolution, which dealt comprehensively with the economic grievances of the middle strata, omitted all mention of the issue in which the workers were particularly interested, namely, the raising of the work norms. The workers were waiting for an additional measure that would give them satisfaction on this point.

They were to be disappointed, however. On June 16, the organ of the Communist trade union federation carried an article informing its readers that the decree on work norms remained in force: the 10 per cent raise was to be carried out by June 30.[8] The effect of this was immediate and drastic. As soon as they read the article, the workers employed on the building sites of the Stalinallee in East Berlin, the showcase of the East German regime, stopped work and marched through the streets of East Berlin to the government headquarters in the Leipziger Strasse. They were joined by thousands on the way; at 1:00 P.M., a huge crowd was assembled in front of the government building. The demonstrators called for the abolition of work norms and the reduction of retail prices. There were also insistent demands for the resignation of Walter Ulbricht, the Communist leader of East Germany, and for free elections in a reunified Germany. The political police did not intervene. Spokesmen of the government, in an effort to calm the demonstrators, announced that the Council of Ministers had rescinded the norm decree.

The demonstrations, however, continued throughout the day. On the following day, June 17, the insurrection became general. The builders' union declared a strike, and most of the other industrial unions followed suit. Berlin was nearly paralyzed, and the streets were filled with marching crowds. The Soviet military commander declared a state of emergency, and tanks were used to disperse the crowds.

Large-scale revolts took place also in the other industrial centers of the East Zone (including Halle, Magdeburg, Leipzig, Merseburg, Dresden, Chemnitz, Erfurt, Kottbus, and Warnemünde). The workers attacked police headquarters and stormed prisons, liberating political prisoners. There were clashes also on some collective farms. Everywhere, the insurrections were put down by Soviet tanks and Communist police. There were many dead.[9]

GERMAN-HUNGARIAN PARALLELS

There is a striking parallelism in the direct procedures by which the Soviet center imposed the New Course upon the Hungarian and East German Communist regimes in June 1953. In both cases, the local Party was forced to admit in public the fundamental error of its past policy; in both, a detailed reform program was dictated by Moscow. The reforms in the two countries were similar in nature, in that they followed the lines of a latter-day NEP, with emphasis upon concessions to the peasantry and small retail trade and upon the mitigation of judicial and police terror.

There were some differences in detail. In Budapest a new premier was appointed, while in East Germany the composition of the government was not changed. On the other hand, the self-critical resolution that the East German Politburo had been forced to adopt was published in full, whereas the Hungarian Central Committee's resolution remained secret (only a toned-down summary of it was given in the speech which the new premier, Nagy, delivered in parliament).

As to the political effect of the Soviet intervention, it was similar in the two countries to the extent that it severely damaged the prestige of both government and Party. In other respects, however, it was dissimilar. In Hungary, the announcement of the New Course calmed the urban population, while it stimulated direct action by the peasants against the kolkhozes whose dissolution had been authorized in principle. In East Germany, no decollectivization of farm land was promised, but the independent farmers received concessions which reassured them; there were only sporadic disorders on collective farms. The East German NEP reforms, however, entirely overlooked the crucial question of the work norms, and the discrepancy between the government's general retreat in all other fields and its refusal to yield on labor policy precipitated industrial rebellion.

The East German uprising itself had many aspects that were to be closely paralleled in the "mass pattern" of the Hungarian Revolution about three years later. In both cases, mass revolt was entirely spontaneous and unorganized, the outgrowth of a street demonstration that had attracted large crowds. Admittedly, the origin of the initial demonstration in each case was different, in that the Berlin demonstrators were workers protesting against output norms, whereas the Budapest students of 1956 staged a peaceful sympathy demonstration cheering the political transformation in Warsaw. In both cities, however, the crowds' demands were similar, that is, they were partly economic and partly political; the people demanded not only better living conditions but also a free regime. In both cases, there were attacks on prisons, police, and Party headquarters; emblems of the Communist regimes were destroyed, and political prisoners released. In both cases, finally, industrial strikes were a central element in the popular resistance.

In many important respects, however, the mass pattern of the Hungarian Revolution differed from the East German uprising. It was far more vehement and radical. In East Germany, there was no concentrated, violent assault upon the political police; there were no lynchings. Above all, the rebellious mass did not set up its own organs of government; no "revolutionary councils" were formed to take over civil administration. The emphasis seems to have been more on specific labor grievances and less on general political demands. Neither in Berlin nor in Budapest did the street crowds try to storm government headquarters; but in Budapest they insisted upon, and obtained, the nomination of their candidate as premier, whereas in Berlin they merely called for the removal of Ulbricht without even proposing a new head of government. (Of course, the Berlin crowds were interested in reunification rather than in a reformed East German government.) Finally, in East Germany, by contrast to Hungary, no attempt was made to organize military resistance against the Soviet occupation troops.

A major difference between Berlin 1953 and Budapest 1956 was the total absence of a revolutionary "elite pattern" in the former. The upper ranks of the East German Party were not divided either by far-reaching policy differences or by the memory of sanguinary purges. Not that the SED was a totally homogeneous, monolithic body. In East Germany as elsewhere in the bloc, there was the usual differentiation between returning "Muscovites" and Communists with a domestic-underground or Western-*émigré* background, and also that between "old" and "new" Party members. Like the other satellite Communist parties, the East German "Socialist Unity Party" was the result of a forced amalgamation of Communists and Social Democrats, and the merger produced considerable friction. All this, however, had little effect upon the top leadership.

The wave of satellite purges touched off by the conflict with Tito and by the Rajk trial in Budapest swept through the East German Communist Party too, but the purge there was infinitely less severe than in Hungary. In August 1950, a few second-rank functionaries were expelled from the Party or deprived of their Party offices. They had become suspect because they were members of a group who during the Nazi regime had emigrated to Western countries, rather than to the Soviet Union, and had had some contact with the American social worker and Party member Noel Field, arrested in Prague on the weird charge of being an agent of American capitalism. Three members of the group were arrested in 1950. The most prominent one, Paul Merker, who had been active in Jewish circles in the emigration, was left at liberty at first, but his turn to be arrested came in 1952, when the "Zionist" label came into use as one designating internal enemies within the Party. The Zionist charge brought Rudolf Slansky, the former Secretary General of the Czechoslovak Communist Party, to the scaffold; Merker was released after a few years in prison. The other Party functionaries implicated in the 1950 affair were not only released but also fully rehabilitated.[10]

No real policy differences were involved in the mild purge of 1950; the action against the victims was based on their unfortunate background rather than on any opposition activity on their part. Even so, the purge could have permanently damaged the situation within the Party if it had been as wide in scope and conducted with as much murderous treachery as were the Hungarian purges of the time. The East German apparatus, however, steered clear of the terroristic excesses that characterized intra-Party purges in the other satellite countries. Thus, the foremost divisive factor in Communist elites, moral outrage at terror and treachery against Party members, was not present in East Germany.

Some minor friction, to be sure, existed at all times. There was personal rivalry between the Party's First Secretary, Walter Ulbricht, and the Politburo member Fritz Dahlem, which caused the latter's temporary eclipse between 1953 and 1957. This affair was a tempest in a teapot. A more serious antileadership movement, however, arose in connection with the economic crisis of 1953. Two leading Party members, Wilhelm Zaisser, the Minister of State Security and a Politburo member, and Rudolf Herrnstadt, the editor-in-chief of the Party newspaper *Neues Deutschland* and a Politburo candidate, organized a cabal in top Party circles in the spring of 1953 with the purpose of deposing Ulbricht (the chief exponent of the hard Stalinist line) and changing the Party's course. The rebels' program was analogous to Nagy's "NEP" line (concessions to the independent farmers; priority for consumer goods). In Soviet Russia, Beria was pushing a similar program, and Zaisser reportedly had several conferences behind the Politburo's back with special emissaries sent by Beria. The rebels also won over a few members of the East German Politburo.

The action against Ulbricht was short-circuited by the revolt of June 17. Ulbricht took the offensive against the rebels at the fifteenth plenary meeting of the Central Committee (July 24–26), the second such meeting called after the revolt. Since the June outbreak had compromised the Party reformers, Ulbricht had the upper hand; he obtained the expulsion of Zaisser and

Herrnstadt from the Central Committee and the Politburo, and the dismissal of Mrs. Else Zaisser from her office of Minister of Education. Other Party members who were implicated also got away with relatively slight penalties. There was no question of exemplary purges and show trials; in view of the strained situation, Moscow favored leniency toward Party members.[11]

Finally, disaffection among Communist intellectuals played no role in preparing the terrain for the uprising of June 1953. This is not surprising; throughout the Soviet bloc, including Hungary, the critical spirit among Communist intellectuals began to manifest itself only after Stalin's death and the inauguration of the New Course.

Thus, the Berlin revolt was essentially a "mass" phenomenon like the Plzen uprising that preceded it. Division within the Communist leadership played a part only to the extent that the sharp censure of the Party and the government which the Politburo issued under strong pressure from the Kremlin helped trigger the revolt. This censure reflected not so much a well-defined alignment of opposing tendencies within the local Communist Party as the temporary ascendancy of Malenkov and Beria in Moscow, and a recognition of the fact that the economic crisis could now no longer be glossed over. The rebellious workers received no positive encouragement from highly placed opposition or reforming elements. The only stimuli from above were the image of a weakened leadership as revealed by retreat and self-denunciation, and the provocation of the norm decree.

In Hungary, the ultimate outbreak of mass revolt had different antecedents, including great power struggles within the leadership and agitation in the public media. Direct outrage and provocation were absent; when the masses turned upon the regime, this was a sudden release of long-pent-up feelings of bitterness and frustration, rather than the effect of some new imposition. In Poland, we observe a similar profile of events during the post-Stalin period: no disorderly incidents in 1953, but a chronic crisis within the leadership resulting in a turbulent, near-revolutionary finale in 1956.

THE POWER STRUGGLE IN POLAND

The internal history of the Polish Communist Party differed from that of the other satellite Communist Parties from the very beginning.[12] In the Polish Party, for example, the Muscovite group of leaders (Boleslaw Bierut, Hilary Minc, Jacob Berman, and others) failed to establish exclusive dominance after the entry of Soviet troops in 1944–45. The indigenous underground, led by Wladyslaw Gomulka, secured one of the decisive power positions in the Party. Gomulka became Secretary General, and his associates Zenon Kliszko, Loga-Sowinski, and Marian Spychalski occupied other key posts in the apparatus. Although the Muscovites in Poland as elsewhere had Stalin's full support, it took several years of strenuous effort before they were able to unseat Gomulka and his associates. During this period, Gomulka consistently upheld his policy of a specifically "Polish road to socialism." Especially as regards the collectivization of agriculture, he took a stand similar to that of Nagy in Hungary.[13] He also championed the internal autonomy and independence of the Polish Communist Party. This was bound to lead to a conflict with the Muscovite element after Stalin launched his drive for the establishment of one-party regimes in the satellite bloc and the complete subordination of the local parties to Moscow's leadership and supervision.

This new line was launched with the creation of the Cominform at a meeting of the leaders of the principal European Communist parties at Szklarska Poreba, in Polish Silesia, in September 1947. Zhdanov, representing the Soviet Union, called for complete coordination and cohesion in the international movement; the Yugoslav Party fully supported him. Gomulka, however, held out for his "Polish road to socialism."[14]

For about a year, Gomulka continued to defend his position publicly, making use of his authority as Secretary General. The rift between the Cominform and the Yugoslav Party, however, eventually made his position untenable. Although his "national Communism" was by no means Titoist in inspiration (in fact, he had worked out his "nationalist" position when Tito himself was a radical internationalist and supporter of Zhdanov's Cominform line), it made him extremely vulnerable after the Yugoslavs veered over to a nationalist line and challenged Moscow on this issue. As the conflict with Yugoslavia intensified, Gomulka at first attempted a slow holding action, and then capitulated altogether.

In the summer of 1948, Gomulka succeeded in staving off the forced merger of the Social Democratic Party with the Communist Party; at the Central Committee meeting of July 7, at which the Cominform's anti-Tito resolution was discussed, he perfunctorily condemned the Tito heresy but still refused to give in on the issue of collectivization. All this made him thoroughly suspect in Moscow's eyes, and his Muscovite arch-rival, Bierut, was able to turn the Central Committee against him. After nearly two months' preparation, the Committee met again on August 31, to judge Gomulka as a "deviationist." Gomulka offered his resignation without defending his position with his customary zeal. Being a Party man first and foremost, he saw no point in arguing his position when he knew that he did not have a majority.[15] He did not, however, pretend that he was converted; in this respect, his behavior differed from that of a typical *apparatchik*.

Once Bierut had wrested the position of Secretary General from Gomulka, the Polish regime quickly adopted the standard policies of the Sovietized one-party state. The merger of the two workers' parties took place in December 1948, six months after the Hungarian merger. Gomulka and his associates were expelled from the Party in January 1949. With this, the stage was set for the purge of the indigenous Party element, the former underground. The first to be arrested were Gomulka's military associates, General Marian Spychalski, Marshal Michal Rola-Zymierski, and General Waclaw Komar; they were tortured in an effort to make them furnish incriminating material against Gomulka. There were numerous other arrests, including those of Gomulka's political supporters Zenon Kliszko and Wladyslaw Bienkowski. Gomulka himself was reportedly arrested at Krynica on August 1, 1951.[16]

It was generally expected that Gomulka would go on trial and suffer the fate of his counterparts in other satellite countries, but no trial was ever held. According to Karol, Bierut deliberately dragged out the preparations for the trial until the whole affair could be forgotten.[17] The Polish purge pattern, on the whole, was different from the Czechoslovak or Hungarian one: there was much treachery and cruelty in the form of false arrests and tortures, but no prominent political or military figure was executed, and no intellectuals were liquidated.

With Gomulka out of the way, the Polish Stalinists embarked upon the prescribed policy of forced industrialization and collectivization. (The latter, however, made much less headway here than in other satellite countries, partly because of stubborn resistance from the peasants and partly because the Polish Stalinists were not quite so extreme in applying coercion as their counterparts in other parts of the bloc.) The over-all economic consequences of the policy were about the same as elsewhere: excessive investment in new industrial construction generated strong inflationary pressures, and the people's standard of living declined. Because of the less strained agricultural situation, however, the 1953 crisis was not as acute in Poland as in Hungary or East Germany. A retreat from the excessive goals of planned industrialization began only in the fall of 1953. In general policy, too, things moved very slowly. While Imre

Nagy was made Premier in Hungary, his Polish counterpart, Gomulka, remained in prison.

Developments within the Polish Communist Party, however, were destined to take a critical turn before long. Revelations about police brutalities made by Jozef Swiatlo, a high-ranking police official who had defected to the West, became known to the Polish public in September 1954 through broadcasts and leaflets emanating from the Free Europe Committee. The revelations, which threw a horrifying light upon the depraved practices of the Communist police state, produced an extraordinary shock effect. At a secret two-day meeting of the Central Party *Aktiv* in December, the Politburo, vehemently denounced by indignant Party members, found itself isolated.[18] The scandal forced the leadership to proceed to a thorough reorganization of the security apparatus. The Central Committee, meeting late in January 1955, dismantled the entire political police apparatus as it had existed until then. The Office of Security (U.B.) was abolished, and security matters were entrusted to a committee; the Minister of Public Security, Radkiewicz, was shunted off to the Ministry of State Farms. The chief police functionaries (the Deputy Minister of Public Security, Roman Romkowski; the head of Department X in the U.B., Anatole Fejgin; and the chief of Judicial Inquiry, Jacek Rozanski) were expelled from the Party and handed over to the courts for punishment.[19] After the abolition of the Office of Security, police practices became much more lenient. The "thaw" had the immediate result that a critical spirit began to manifest itself in the public media. In Poland, as later in Hungary, the Party intellectuals were the first to attack the regime's shortcomings. Critical writings began to appear first, in the autumn of 1954, in the periodicals controlled by the Communist writers' organization (*Nowa kultura* and *Po prostu*). In the spring of 1955, the intellectuals began organizing private discussion clubs, the first of which, launched in Warsaw, was named "Club of the Crooked Circle."[20] But whereas in Hungary there was no real volume of public criticism until after the Twentieth Congress of the CPSU in February 1956, the Polish Communist periodical press and also the daily newspaper *Trybuna ludu* (the organ of the Central Committee) carried a good deal of criticism of the official policy and printed demands for liberalization throughout 1955. Non-Communist literary figures who had been silenced but whose voices commanded respect also began to appear in print. This relative freedom of discussion in Poland was a unique phenomenon in the Communist bloc at that time.

Ferment in public opinion gradually discredited the Polish Stalinist leadership, and the comeback of the Gomulka wing became the dominant political issue. Gomulka himself was released from prison late in 1954, in the wake of the Swiatlo affair, but was first banished to the countryside. After the Twentieth Congress, however, the question of his return to political activity became acute. The Party opposition's demands for economic reforms and liberalization now became overwhelmingly insistent. As in Hungary, the rehabilitation of former purge victims led to sharp intra-Party debates, and the question of responsibility was aired. Criticism of the regime's cultural policies, notably of the officially imposed line of "socialist realism," swelled to a veritable flood. On the political scene, there were unprecedented stirrings of activity. The Polish parliament, formerly a rubber-stamp body, came to life. The government invited parliamentary criticism and received heavy doses of it at the session of April 23–28, 1956.

At the same time, the industrial masses also became active. Many mass meetings were held in May, encouraged by the Central Committee; there were insistent demands for comprehensive reforms and also for Gomulka's recall from exile. The mounting storm of criticism forced a change in the composition of the government; early in May, Jacob Berman, a leading Stalinist, was dropped from the Politburo and forced to abandon his post of Assistant Premier.

The position of Secretary General of the Party had been taken over in the meantime by the Stalinist Edward Ochab, approved by Khrushchev to succeed Bierut, who had died in Moscow while attending the Twentieth Congress. Ochab tried to hold the line, but had to recognize that the situation in the country made this impossible. The regime, indeed, received a sharp warning: on June 28, the workers of Poznan rose in revolt. The events in Poznan were similar in many respects to the Berlin uprising of three years before. The workers of the ZISPO plant (the ZIS automotive plant in Poznan) went on strike and staged a mass demonstration; workers from other plants followed suit. The demonstrators stormed police stations and obtained arms. They called for bread and the withdrawal of Soviet troops from Poland. Soldiers of the conscript army fraternized with the people. The crowds were finally dispersed by Polish security forces riding in tanks, and order was restored after a state of emergency had been declared. According to official sources, 38 persons were killed and 270 wounded; private estimates of the casualties put the figures much higher.[21]

The internal crisis in the Party developed rapidly after Poznan. At the Seventh Plenum of the Central Committee in July, the opposition demanded Gomulka's rehabilitation and readmission to the Party, together with far-reaching economic and political reforms. The Central Committee thereupon decided to make certain concessions to the independent peasants and the industrial workers, but the newly elected Politburo was still overwhelmingly Stalinist in its composition. Nevertheless, shortly after the Plenum, Gomulka and two of his supporters, Spychalski and Kliszko, who had also been expelled from the Party and imprisoned, were readmitted to the Party, and the position of the Gomulka wing thereafter became stronger and stronger. Late in August, the newly rehabilitated Kliszko was named Assistant Minister of Justice, and another purge victim, General Komar, was appointed head of the internal security forces. In September, a full-fledged Party schism became manifest: the extreme Stalinists deliberated among themselves at Natolin, while the Party opposition conducted separate discussions at Pulawy.

The political tide was running strongly against Natolin. The more moderate Stalinists, notably Gomulka's erstwhile antagonist, Edward Ochab, recognized that the regime could be saved only by taking over Gomulka's program of making concessions to the peasantry and relaxing Russia's grip on Poland, and by handing the leadership over to him. The Politburo reached an agreement with Gomulka on this basis in mid-October. Sensing its isolation, the Natolin group was sending urgent appeals to Moscow, warning against the impending changes. Alarmed by the developments in Poland, Moscow tried to arbitrate between the opposing factions, inviting the Polish Party leadership to a conference in Moscow. The Polish Politburo, however, declined the invitation, arguing that the Central Committee plenum, scheduled for October 19, could not be postponed.

The Eighth Plenum of the Central Committee met on the prearranged date in an atmosphere of acute crisis. Moscow made a last-minute attempt to prevent the rout of the Natolinites: Khrushchev, Mikoyan, Molotov, and Kaganovich flew to Warsaw to address the meeting in person and to offer counsels of moderation backed up by massive threats.

Indeed, while the meeting was in session, things in the country were moving toward an armed clash. Preparations for a *coup* by Natolin, to be supported by military force, had become known on the eve of the meeting. The workers' factory guards, who had been in readiness to defend the impending reforms, mobilized themselves to meet the threat. On the other side, Soviet motorized troops began moving from Silesia in the direction of Warsaw. The Polish security forces and regular army were ready for resistance.[22]

The Central Committee, in its turn, went through with the

reshuffling of the Party leadership as planned. It was Ochab who proposed the election of Gomulka and three of his associates (Spychalski, Kliszko, and Loga-Sowinski) to the Central Committee. Moscow's representatives finally acquiesced in the changes. The prospect of armed conflict was unpalatable to them, and the Poles were able to reassure them about their future policy. Thus, the tension subsided before the meeting was over.

Marshal Rokossowski, the former Soviet army chief who had stayed in Poland as Defense Minister and Politburo member, told the Central Committee that Marshal Konev, commander of Soviet troops in Poland, had reassured him that no further troop movements would take place. The earlier movements, he said, had only been "routine maneuvers," and Polish fears about Soviet armed intervention were unfounded. Gomulka, in turn, adopted a conciliatory tone toward Russia in his speech in the Central Committee.

Thus, the leadership passed to Gomulka with the Russians' blessing. On October 21, the Central Committee elected a new Politburo in which Gomulka and his supporters had the edge over the Stalinist group; Gomulka was made Secretary General of the Communist Party, while Marshal Rokossowski and the Stalinist Zenon Nowak were dropped.

The victory of the Party opposition aroused tremendous popular enthusiasm. A new, freer era seemed at hand. The masses in Warsaw and other Polish cities were jubilant. Gomulka was hailed as a genuine national leader; people acknowledged the transformation achieved under his leadership as Poland's "spring in October."

Gomulka's first measures indeed put into effect the Party opposition's reform program. The collectivization drive was stopped, and centralized economic controls were relaxed. Labor, represented by workers' councils, acquired a share in the management of plants. An accord was concluded with the

Church, restoring religious freedom. Intellectual freedom, too, was respected. Relations with Soviet Russia were put on a new basis: Poland's independent status was confirmed in principle, and it was agreed that the Soviet armed forces in Poland would not interfere in the country's internal affairs.

The Communist Party rebels expected these changes to herald a great revival: freed from the excesses and aberrations of the Stalin era, the Party would command the genuine loyalty of all the productive strata of the population and hence would be able to function as the guiding organ of a truly popular government. Subsequent developments, however, proved that these expectations were illusory. The experiment of factory self-management proved a failure; it turned out that the system could function only on the basis of centralized economic controls. It was also impossible to maintain freedom of public discussion. If the Gomulka experiment demonstrated anything, it was that the one-party regime could not survive without the regimentation of public opinion. The same held true as regards relations between the bloc countries and Russia; the local Communists were unable to function without the centralized control of Moscow. The Soviet Union reasserted its dominance; the transformation of the satellite empire into a free community of nations was just a wishful dream.

POLISH-HUNGARIAN PARALLELS

Comparing the elite pattern of the Polish upheaval with that of the Hungarian Revolution, we are struck by two basic similarities. In both countries, a "right-wing" Party group opposed the Stalinists, advocating a NEP-like policy and the liberalization of public life. In both, the Party's intellectual spokesmen, the Communist writers, played a decisive role in bringing these ideas before the public and discrediting the Stalinist Old Guard.

There were also, however, important differences between

143

the two elite patterns: during the crucial months preceding the October events, intra-Party developments in Poland and Hungary diverged sharply.

First of all, polarization in the Polish Communist Party began earlier and was more sharply defined than in the Hungarian. When Imre Nagy was first advocating the NEP line, he was isolated in the Party; Gomulka, however, was an entrenched leader, and it was not without difficulty that the Stalinists eventually eliminated him and his followers from the leadership. During the early controversies on industrialization and collectivization, Nagy was not able to challenge Rákosi forcefully; later, he submitted to Rákosi and kept his ideas to himself. It was the Moscow center that propelled Nagy into a leading position when, during the early New Course period, it decided to introduce a NEP policy in Hungary. The Hungarian Party's polarization into two opposing camps had its origin in the dual control situation engineered by Moscow, with Rákosi at the head of the Party apparatus and Nagy at the head of the governmental bureaucracy. In Poland, by contrast, Gomulka had strong roots in the apparatus itself. When the deterioration of the political situation forced the leadership to readmit Gomulka and his supporters, the Gomulka group were able to bid successfully for the restoration of their former power.

The personality factor also enters into the picture. Gomulka was a hard fighter, thoroughly inured to the dog-eat-dog atmosphere in the apparatus. He concentrated upon first taking possession of control positions; the time to debate issues would come after this was achieved. Nagy was a different kind of person. Essentially a lawyer, he was interested above all in proving his point. Once this was done, he was glad to let the apparatus—his superiors in Budapest and Moscow—make the decisions. The apparatus, he felt, could not fail to make the right decision once the truth had been demonstrated. With this basic attitude, Nagy was not the man to force the hand of intensely power-hungry opponents such as Rákosi and Gerö. In addition, the issues separating the Party reformers from the Old Guard, though basically similar in the two countries, were much more intractable in Hungary. In agriculture, for example, the Hungarian regime was faced with the problem of retreating from the level of collectivization already reached, with 39.2 per cent of the arable land belonging to kolkhozes and sovkhozes. In Poland, where only about 9 per cent of the land was collectivized and most of the kolkhozes were in the newly acquired western provinces, the main thing was to stop the collectivization drive and help independent farmers.

Personalities and economic issues, however, were not the focal elements in the Hungarian intra-Party crisis. What poisoned the atmosphere more than anything else was the memory of the great purges. The Hungarian purges were far more vicious and savage than the Polish ones. The latter, too, involved inhuman terror on a large scale, but, within the Party at least, they stopped short of the Hungarian excesses. Gomulka was treated roughly, but his life as well as his dignity was spared; the leaders of the Polish intra-Party opposition were not hanged for mythical crimes to which they had been forced to confess. Moreover, the Polish Communist leaders who bore the main responsibility for the terror were gradually eliminated from prominent positions, whereas in Hungary the main culprit was the Party leader, Rákosi, himself, and he regained undisputed supremacy after his temporary eclipse during the New Course. Thus, the rehabilitation of the Hungarian victims of terror did not include calling their persecutors to account. The Hungarian Old Guard's attempts to shake off responsibility by laying the purges at the door of the police were unavailing; a reconciliation with the Party opposition was impossible. In Poland, by contrast, the Old Guard could bow to the Gomulka wing and accept a diminished position in the recognized leadership. Stalinists, like Ochab, were able to cross the line. It was thus possible to end the Party schism and create a cohesive leadership at the last moment. In Hungary, only the complete elimination of the Old Guard would do, but the opposition was not strong enough to achieve this. The schism could not be healed.

Let us now compare the mass pattern of the revolutionary periods in Poland and Hungary. Developments in this respect followed a totally dissimilar course in the two countries. In Poland, there was no sudden, explosive change from total quiescence to total insubordination. Considerable mass activity had preceded the October climax. Not only did the ferment in public opinion stirred up by intellectuals thus have a longer time in which to act upon the public mind, but the Polish political authorities themselves encouraged the masses to become politically active and express their feelings. The mass disturbance in Poland in the spring and summer of 1956, culminating in the Poznan riot, was a genuine "thaw" effect, or rather, as in East Germany three years before, the joint effect of relaxation and of pent-up and acute grievances. The Poznan events, which revealed in a flash the full extent of bitterness in the working class, served as a salutary warning to the regime. The Poznan uprising more than anything else convinced the Old Guard that a radical change was inevitable.

There was considerable mass activity in Poland during the crucial October days: mass meetings, formation of workers' councils, organization of factory guards. The aroused masses, however, ranged themselves behind Gomulka's leadership. The street crowds did not get out of hand, because the regime had convinced the people that their basic demands would be met. In Hungary, on the other hand, the Communist regime had been vainly groping for a solution during the critical summer months. The quiescence of the masses had lulled the Party leadership and its Moscow overlords into a false sense of security. After Rákosi's removal in July, a slow, gradual process of transformation seemed the safest course. The power-holders did not know how totally embittered the people had become. This was revealed only when the street crowds suddenly rose in rebellion on the evening of October 23. Just as in Berlin in June 1953, it was by then too late to disarm the people by political concessions. The masses took things into their own hands.

One difference between the two countries was particularly crucial. The Polish Communist leaders were clearly aware—as their Hungarian counterparts, with the exception of Nagy, were not—that, insofar as the people were concerned, the main issue was not internal reform but the Soviet occupation. Realizing this, Gomulka, upon seizing power, concentrated upon measures designed to convince the people that the Soviets' grip over Poland was being relaxed: he forced the removal of Soviet Marshal Rokossowski from the Polish Politburo and promised a change in Polish-Soviet relations. Had he not done so, the chances are that the Polish workers' council movement, like the Hungarian, would have proclaimed a strike against the Soviet occupation. In the end, to be sure, Poland's gains in the matter of national independence turned out to be extremely modest. But Gomulka's show of self-assertion against the Soviets enabled him to retain his control over the masses. Nagy in Hungary lost control mainly because he was unable to start his premiership with a similar national gesture. (On the contrary, it was given out that he, Nagy, had invited Soviet troops to restore order in Budapest).[23]

There is tragic irony in all this, because Nagy, as his book shows, was intensely concerned about national independence.[24] He was a genuine patriot. But his first acts in office did not reveal this, and most of the other Hungarian Communists, whether they were for or against Rákosi, failed to recognize the importance of the national issue. As a result, the Hungarian masses refused to take guidance from any Communist, even Nagy and the antiregime intellectuals, and claimed all power for their own revolutionary organizations which took an uncompromising stand on national independence and the end of Soviet occupation.

10

CONCLUSIONS

Having considered the Hungarian Revolution and parallel cases, we shall now turn to the general problem of political stability and instability under Communism. The record in fact permits us to identify certain factors that seem to be regularly associated with instability. The question is whether similar factors might assert themselves again in the future in the Soviet bloc, and under what conditions. This concluding chapter will be devoted to a brief, and necessarily speculative, discussion of this problem.

THE EFFECT UPON THE MASSES OF DIVISION WITHIN THE ELITE

The first conclusion that emerges from the data is the critical importance of whether there is division or unity within the top ruling group; indeed, it is a condition determining the chances for open breaches of public order.

How thoroughly alienated all social strata were from the Communist regime became manifest in the East German uprising of June 1953 as well as in the Hungarian Revolution of 1956. We may assume that the people's mood was similar in the other satellite countries, possibly with some mitigation in the case of Czechoslovakia. (The standard of living in that country is higher than elsewhere in the bloc, and there is no military occupation, but, even so, the regime is essentially an alien one.) Major disturbances, however, occurred only in very few instances. By and large, popular resentment, though profound, did not manifest itself openly. The totalitarian control

149

system prevented this by "atomizing" the people, by keeping all expressions of protest out of public media, by making everybody dependent on the central authorities for livelihood, and so on. Protesting in public was not only prohibitively risky but also futile, since no potential alternative to the prevailing system was visible.

All this depended, however, on the maintenance of unity, or at least of a public image of unity, within the governing apparatus. This was generally the case in the stable countries of the bloc. Purges, of course, did occur within their ruling groups, but the existence of any rift was acknowledged only when the deviants had been unmasked and crushed. In none of the stable countries was the blame for bad conditions publicly laid at the door of the Party as a whole or of leaders actually continuing in power. In this respect, East Germany, Hungary, and Poland deviated from the stable countries.

The public discrediting of leading Party members served as a signal that changes of policy were possible, and this impression tended to stir mass protest action. Theoretically, the masses could have passively waited for concessions from above (as they did in the stable countries), but this is not how things worked out in the unstable countries. Open blame directed against top circles diminished the atomization of the people, and some groups within the population sooner or later responded by collective action, aimed at exacting concessions. The main instances of this have been treated in Chapters 3, 8, and 9. Now the question is whether, and in what circumstances, one can expect open division of this type to recur in the Soviet bloc, and, if so, what effect it is likely to have upon the political stability of Communist regimes.

Mere personal and clique rivalries, which inevitably arise in Communist ruling groups, do not seem likely in themselves to produce far-reaching disruptive effects. For one thing, power struggles of a more or less routine kind are usually carried on behind the scenes; for another, they do not, as a rule, involve policy differences of immediate interest to the population. Mass ferment was observed primarily when top-level controversies both discredited a previously all-powerful leader or clique and indicated the regime's willingness to reconsider basic policies and make concessions to popular desires. Such a constellation of circumstances might arise again, for example, if erroneous planning decisions again create acute difficulties that discredit some of the top decision-makers and necessitate a drastic revision of policy. But it must be noted that strongly entrenched leaders are, as a rule, able to avoid blame for the ill effects of erroneous policies and planning decisions. It was only during the protracted succession crisis after Stalin's death that policy changes involving concessions to the population sometimes became a matter of public controversy among leading figures. What the record suggests, then, is that only another succession crisis, in conjunction with acute economic difficulties, is likely to create conditions favorable to open mass protests.

But supposing such protests do occur, the question is, How gravely will they compromise the stability of the regime? In Berlin and Budapest, open mass protests set off a chain reaction, drawing more and more groups into an insurrectionary vortex. Other outbreaks (the peasants' revolts in Hungary and the Poznan uprising, for example) were contained, and order was restored. In both cases, however, open challenges to governmental authority had considerable political aftereffects. This indicates that even isolated disorders can, in conjunction with chronic divisions among the policy-makers, introduce serious factors of instability. In the present context, however, the main question is under what conditions public disorders may assume revolutionary or near-revolutionary dimensions. In this connection, the record shows that "chain reactions" occurred in a constellation similar to that surrounding a number of other "mass revolutions" recorded in modern history.

Conclusions

Whether mass outbreaks could or could not be contained seems to have depended, first and foremost, on the place where they occurred. Order was restored when uprisings took place in the periphery (provincial industrial centers or the countryside). The chain reactions were set off by mass demonstrations in political capitals. It is, of course, only in the capital city that rebellious masses can come into contact with the top authorities themselves. When the capital is in uproar, the physical safety of the rulers is potentially in jeopardy. The opportunity to achieve something politically decisive gives people a unique motivation to join the rebellion; thus, the presence of the government in itself provides a stimulus for a chain reaction.

Not that mass disorders in capital cities always produce such an explosive effect. In the majority of cases, the police or the security forces disperse demonstrating crowds before the situation becomes critical. This is likely to happen when demonstrations take place under the auspices of some organized party or movement voicing specific demands or grievances not shared by other segments of the population. In such cases, the security forces and the challengers face each other as well-delimited, internally cohesive groups, and the odds favor the former. Psychologically, however, the cohesion of the security forces depends on the possibility of marking the challengers off against the national community which the forces are pledged to defend. Unorganized, improvised uprisings that grow spontaneously and in which people from all walks of life participate put the cohesion of the security forces under severe strain. Conscript army units that are being used as security forces to disperse large crowds are particularly vulnerable to this disruptive factor: when soldiers face "the people," they are psychologically disarmed. This is how things have worked out time and again in mass disorders or revolutions. The regular army could not be used as a security force at Plzen, Poznan, or Budapest; and the same thing could be observed in earlier times also. In the Russian February Revolution of 1917, for example, the Petrograd garrison made common cause with the insurgent crowds; a similar phenomenon had occurred in the course of the first modern mass revolt, the assault upon the Bastille in 1789. For governments faced with insurrection in the capital, the critical question ever since 1789 has been whether specially trained and indoctrinated security forces were sufficient to disperse the crowds. Where this was not the case, and regular troops had to be brought in, the government repeatedly found itself without physical protection because the troops refused to fire upon the people, or made common cause with them. Apparently, even totalitarian regimes are subject to this hazard. Their security apparatus can cope with organized opposition, but they cannot rely on the loyalty of their conscript troops in fighting spontaneous mass upheavals. Here is one of the limits of totalitarian power.

This hazard, however, must not be overestimated. As we have observed, open mass protests in totalitarian societies seem to be contingent on specific circumstances, such as rifts of a particularly grave nature within the leadership; moreover, they will not set off a critical chain reaction unless some further conditions are given as well. Spontaneous mass outbreaks are unlikely events: they may be brought about by a peculiar combination of circumstances but cannot be organized and stimulated at will.

There are other types of revolutionary action, however, which do not depend on uncontrollable circumstances but are a matter of deliberate initiative. Terrorism, a frequent modern type of insurrectionary activity, is a case in point. It only takes a fully dedicated core of extreme opponents of a regime to initiate terrorism; given a modicum of resources (which may be supplied from the outside), as well as popular sympathy, terrorism can slowly undermine the prevailing regime and culminate in extensive, endemic guerrilla warfare, even when the bulk of the population is not ready to mobilize itself for open protest action. This terroristic type of revolutionary activity has been observed time and again in our own days; it is sufficient to mention such outstanding examples as Palestine, Cyprus, Algeria, and Cuba. It is noteworthy, however, that major terroristic activity has so far been limited to feebly industrialized colonial or ex-colonial societies. No instances of it have been observed either in the industrialized West or in the Soviet bloc, apart from underground resistance and partisan activity in wartime.

It is not possible to go into the reasons for this variation in the incidence of revolutionary terrorism in different types of society, but the assumption seems justified that endemic terrorism of the colonial type is unlikely to flare up in the Soviet empire in the future, at least as long as basic conditions remain unchanged. As things stand now, spontaneous mass upheavals in capital cities seem to represent the only type of acute threat from below to which Communist regimes are exposed.

But this is not to say that Communist regimes must constantly reckon with climactic outbreaks as a real possibility. Mass revolutions are essentially unpredictable; as observed above, they presuppose an unlikely combination of circumstances. Moreover, the observed trend toward improving mass standards of living may be expected to lessen the probability of mass outbreaks and chain reactions still further.

Material grievances, however, by no means represent the only source of popular protest. As we have seen, national independence rather than improvement of material conditions was the chief goal of the revolutionary masses in Hungary, and this issue will not disappear when life becomes materially more bearable. On the other hand, the Hungarian and Polish events have demonstrated that the satellite nations are too weak to liberate themselves, and that they cannot count upon effective outside help. Also, developments since 1957 have made Soviet Russia's military strength appear in a new, awesome light. For these reasons, the satellite area can no longer be expected to represent the main center of political disturbances in the Soviet bloc, as it did in the post-Stalin crises. Should the political situation again become fluid in the Soviet Union, signs of instability, if any, are more likely to appear in the core area than in the satellite belt.

MORAL AND IDEOLOGICAL REBELLION

In the cases we have observed of grave rifts within Communist elites, the critical factor was the ideological and moral one. Elite disaffection was fanned by feelings that the Party, or its top leadership, had betrayed the cause and that the Party's actual policies ran counter to the ideal of emancipating and elevating the working masses. Police terror against Party members was another source of moral rebellion. Such moral opposition to the Stalinist policies of the top leadership, however, only became a potent force in the unstable countries. It may indeed be assumed that many insiders had had qualms and doubts in the stable bloc countries too, but they somehow had come to terms with them; there was no open rebellion.

To explain this, we have to start from the observation that condemnation of Communist oppression, of the monstrosity of purges, and so on, had been commonplace throughout the Stalin era: outside critics had made these points again and again, and the Communist insiders were aware both of these charges and of the facts that had given rise to them. Their Party schooling, however, had enabled them to explain everything away by dialectical arguments. What looked on the surface like oppression and exploitation in the Communist system was, seen "objectively" in the proper historical context, emancipation and elevation. What looked like blatant personal injustice was "objectively" the highest form of justice. A person had to silence his own qualms and doubts once the Party, through its top authorities, had laid down the correct interpretation of the matter. Before their rebellion, the disaffected insiders in the unstable bloc countries had been thinking along such lines too. Eventually, however, they came to question the validity of the official dialectical interpretation of Party policies; and total rejection became possible when the previously accredited official interpreters of reality were themselves discredited, openly condemned, by the Party's own spokesmen.

The insiders' rebellion, then, involved two things: first, the reassertion of long-suppressed moral feelings and intellectual convictions; second, the breakdown of previously accepted authority relationships. In the case of most Party people, the first was unlikely to occur without the second. Self-assertion and rebellion presupposed the collapse of the image of the leadership as the only authentic interpreter of reality. The political consequences were serious because the Party's "legitimacy," its claim to being accepted as the governing organ of society, is intimately bound up with this interpreting function. In the Communist system, stubborn, unresolved differences among insiders concerning the "scientifically" correct interpretation of reality are tantamount to a constitutional crisis. It is vitally important, for political stability, to resolve such differences, to restore unanimity of outlook within the framework of the Party's ideological tradition. Restoring unanimity is not too difficult when hierarchical relations within the Party are clearly defined and no group of insiders experiences severe moral conflicts. If so, uniform ideological schooling, as well as the common stake all insiders have in maintaining the Party's position, tend to act as powerful forces for unity. In the examples we have observed, inside conflicts were intractable because the basic hierarchical and moral conditions of unity were not satisfied.

Could internal conflicts of a similarly intractable nature

arise in the Party in the future? Hierarchical lines of authority may well become blurred, for example, in another succession crisis. But wrangling about power positions need not have a profoundly unsettling effect. A serious constitutional crisis is likely to arise only when inside groups experience a moral shock, when they are brought face to face with deficiencies, failures, and shortcomings of an intolerable nature in the working of the Party. Such shocks, however, are essentially unpredictable. As long as the regime is successful, moral qualms and ideological criticisms are likely to remain subdued.

At the same time, ideological and moral unity within the Party is apt to undergo a slow, gradual process of disintegration. There is a gap between the regime's ideological commitments and the practical possibilities open to it, a gap that is bound to widen as time goes on. To be sure, material progress, improved supply of consumer goods, better working conditions, and the like make for greater popular acceptance of the system. But the Party cannot be satisfied with this. It is ideologically committed to the far more radical, utopian goal of the total transformation of society, summed up by the slogan "building communism."

Under "communism," not only class distinctions but also other status differences and functional specializations are supposed to disappear; "communism" means, for example, the obliteration of all distinction between manual and intellectual labor as well as the "withering away" of the state and its bureaucratic machinery. In reality, however, the developing and maturing industrial society is organized along lines antithetical to this egalitarian vision. It cannot do without technical and administrative staffs and highly trained specialists, set off from the mass of operatives. To tear down the existing system of specialization and stratification is a practical impossibility. Yet the Party cannot acknowledge that the present articulation of industrial society is here to stay, progress and improvement

157

being possible only within the framework of the *status quo.* To recognize this would be tantamount to admitting that Soviet society is just a variant of the type of industrial civilization that also exists elsewhere. This is incompatible with the Party's definition of its mission, the consummation of the meaning of all history by the creation of a radically new type of society. The political vitality of the Party depends on preserving this sense of mission. But this is difficult to do when actual innovations can only have limited scope.

This discrepancy between the key symbols defining the Party's mission and the available possibilities for practical developmental work is bound to lead to political frustrations and conflicts. If the gap persists, it will give rise to a tendency to devalue the traditional ideology as irrelevant and obsolescent. Vigorous, independent thinkers in the elite are likely to become impatient with being compelled to relate actual developments to a historical vision to which real life stubbornly refuses to conform. Questioning the validity of the Party's key symbols, however, would not be merely a private matter. It would tend to have practical political significance, because political authority in the system depends on whose interpretation of key political symbols is accepted as valid.

The problem can be evaded, as happens, for example, when scientists pay ritualistic homage to the classics of Marxism as a great source of basic insights within their disciplines. This will satisfy the political authorities and leave the scientists free to proceed along independent lines in their substantive work of research, theorizing, and experimentation. But such compromises, based upon mutual mental reservations, are not always possible. Methods of analysis independent of the ideological tradition may lead to conclusions that the political authorities are forced to regard as subversive. When such issues cannot be glossed over, moral conflicts may arise. The opposing sides may feel that they have fundamental values to defend;

both then will claim to represent the "true" ideal of Marxism, and see in their opponent's position a public danger. This type of conflict is unlikely to arise between political authorities and natural scientists; direct political interference with scientific teachings, such as was observed in the Lysenko affair, is not likely to recur. But there are fields more closely related to politics, such as economic analysis, education, or even art and literature, in which younger people, in particular, may feel impelled to cut adrift from ideological orthodoxy, not merely for theoretical reasons but also for reasons of public welfare. As the Party's ideological heritage becomes obsolescent, this type of conflict is more and more likely to come to the fore.

The ideological and moral conflicts that may arise in this way within the Soviet elite in the future would in all probability lack the intensity of the satellite conflicts discussed above, so that they would not be likely to have the same explosive consequences. But if positions defended with deep moral and ideological conviction clash, the political consequences are nevertheless bound to be serious in the long run, involving shifts in authority relationships as well as more or less far-reaching institutional and ideological changes. It cannot be predicted with any certainty whether constitutional crises of this sort will occur in the Soviet area, or how gravely they might endanger the stability of the political system. But sources of moral conflict do exist; indeed moral conflicts causing rifts within the political elites may be said to pose the most immediate potential threat to the political stability of Communist regimes.

NOTES

Full titles and publication data are given only for works not listed in the Bibliography.

NOTES TO CHAPTER ONE

1. In East Germany, too, the retreat occurred in abrupt fashion, with explosive results (see Chapter 9).

NOTES TO CHAPTER TWO

1. On this period, see "Le Peuple hongrois contre le communisme," *Est et Ouest*, special issue, October 16–31, 1957, pp. 15ff.
2. *Est et Ouest*, p. 17.
3. Imre Kovács, *Im Schatten der Sowjets*, Zurich, 1948, pp. 26f. Kovács adds that he found out soon afterward that the Communist Party had only "a few hundred" followers at that time.
4. *Ibid.*, pp. 208f.
5. *Est et Ouest*, p. 23.
6. See pp. 101f., below.
7. For a detailed account, see Nagy, *The Struggle Behind the Iron Curtain*, Part IV; and Healey, *The Curtain Falls*.
8. Zbigniew Brzezinski, "The Pattern of Political Purges," *The Annals of the American Academy of Political and Social Science*, CCCXVII (1958), 84 (hereafter quoted as *The Annals*).
9. A critical account of the Rajk trial, pointing out the inconsistencies and absurdities in the prosecution's case, is found in Fejtö, *La Tragédie hongroise*, pp. 60–78 (omitted from the English translation of Fejtö's book). See also Vladimir Dedijer, *Tito*, New York, 1953, pp. 393ff.
10. Accounts of Communist methods of building up cases against undesirable elements are found in Kovago, *You Are All Alone*, and Ignotus, *Political Prisoner*.
11. Fejtö, *Behind the Rape of Hungary*, p. 12.

12. Speech by Mátyás Rákosi, *The Way of Our People's Democracy,* published in English translation by the National Committee for a Free Europe, Research and Publication Service, New York, May 1952, pp. 6f.

13. Quoted in Paul Fábry's Introduction to Rákosi's Academy speech, *ibid.*

14. Robert Gabor, "Organization and Strategy of the Hungarian Workers' (Communist) Party," National Committee for a Free Europe, Research and Publication Services, New York, July 1952, p. 11.

15. This term is taken from Brzezinski in *The Annals* (1958), p. 85. On the post-Stalin police purges, see below, pp. 74, 138.

16. *Imre Nagy on Communism,* English translation of *Nagy Imre A Nép Védelmében* (Imre Nagy in Defense of the People), Budapest, 1957. The Hungarian original bears the imprint "Revolutionary Council." It appears to have been published clandestinely after the Soviet intervention.

17. *Ibid.,* p. 195. 18. *Ibid.,* p. 198. 19. *Ibid.*

20. Dezsö Nemes, "Revizionism i kontrrevolutsiia v Vengrii" (Revisionism and Counterrevolution in Hungary), *Novaia i noveishaia Istoriia* (Modern and Contemporary History), No. 6 (November 1958), pp. 16–26. I am indebted to Myron Rush for bringing this source to my attention and translating the main passages of the article from the Russian.

21. *Ibid.,* p. 17. 22. *Ibid.,* p. 18 . 19. *Ibid.*

24. See Nagy's biography in Helmreich (ed.), *Hungary,* p. 402.

25. *Ibid.,* p. 17.

26. Meray, *Thirteen Days That Shook the Kremlin,* p. 16.

NOTES TO CHAPTER THREE

1. Nicolas Spulber, "The Development of Industry," *The Annals,* CCCXVII (1958), 40.

2. A deliberately vague summary of the Soviet leaders' denunciation of Rákosi is found in *Imre Nagy on Communism,* p. 66; a fuller account is given in Meray, *Thirteen Days,* pp. 3–9. See also Kecskemeti, "Limits and Problems of Decompression," *The Annals* (1958), pp. 97–106.

3. Meray, *Thirteen Days,* p. 7.

4. The complete text of Nagy's speech appeared in the Party's daily newspaper, *Szabad Nép* (Free People), July 5, 1953.

5. Personal interview.

6. *Szabad Nép,* July 10 and 11, 1953.

7. *Ibid.,* July 12, 1953.

8. *Imre Nagy on Communism,* p. 143. A former Communist official gave the same information in a personal interview.

9. Meray, *Thirteen Days*, p. 25; see also *Imre Nagy on Communism*, p. 176.

10. Meray, *Thirteen Days*, p. 22.

11. The text of the resolution is in *Szabad Nép*, March 9, 1955.

12. Meray, *Thirteen Days*, p. 29.

13. *Ibid.*, p. 51.

NOTES TO CHAPTER FOUR

1. See pp. 9ff. above.

2. Révai made these remarks in a speech delivered at the Cultural Congress of the Hungarian Communist Party in October 1952. For a French translation of the passage referred to, see *Les Temps Modernes*, XII (special issues on the Hungarian Revolution), 796ff.

3. Personal interview.

4. This motif is frequent in dissident Communist literature; see, for example, Milovan Djilas, *The New Class*, New York, 1958, pp. 152 and 154f.

5. *Irodalmi Ujság* (Literary Gazette), August 1, 1953.

6. Published in *Irodalmi Ujság*, August 1, 1953; reprinted in István Csicsery-Ronáy, *Költök Forradalma* (A Revolution of Poets), Washington, 1959, p. 15.

7. *Irodalmi Ujság*, November 7, 1953; reprinted in *Költök Forradalma*, pp. 16–21.

8. See above, pp. 44ff.

9. Poem "Igy Vagyunk" (That's How We Are), written on September 3, 1955, published in *Béke és Szabadság* (Peace and Freedom), June 27, 1956; French translation in *Les Temps Modernes*, XII, 887f.

10. Gyula Sipos, "Szorongás" (Anxiety), *Irodalmi Ujság*, July 7, 1956; reprinted in *Költök Forradalma*, pp. 44f.

11. Zoltán Zelk, "Feltámadás" (Resurrection), *Irodalmi Ujság*, August 4, 1956; reprinted in *Költök Forradalma*, pp. 48f.

12. Peter Kuczka, "Inkább Meztelen" (Rather Walk Naked), *Irodalmi Ujzág*, September 8, 1956; reprinted in *Költök Forradalma*, p. 62.

13. "Töredék" (Fragment), *Irodalmi Ujság*, July 28, 1956; reprinted in *Költök Forradalma*, p. 47.

14. *Uj Hang* (New Voice), October 1956; reprinted in *Költök Forradalma*, p. 66.

15. *Irodalmi Ujság*, June 30, 1956.

16. "Egyetlen Élet" (But One Life), *Irodalmi Ujság*, September 24, 1955; reprinted in *Költök Forradalma*, p. 25.

17. *Irodalmi Ujság*, October 6, 1956; French translation in *Les Temps Modernes*, XII, 843–46.

18. *Ibid.*, p. 849.
19. *Les Temps Modernes* (*loc. cit.*) gives the number of signatories as 63; whereas Meray (*Thirteen Days*, p. 39) speaks of 59 signatures.
20. An account of these developments was given to me by Aczél in a personal interview.
21. Personal interview.
22. See Paul Kecskemeti, "Intellectual Unrest Behind the Iron Curtain," *Commentary*, XXIV (1957), 400. The same point was brought out by a Hungarian ex-Communist writer who had been imprisoned in the Rajk purge and escaped from Hungary after the 1956 revolution: Vincent Savarius (pseud.), "The Vicissitudes and Conflicts of Moralizing Elements in the Soviet Theory and Practice," *The Review*, Quarterly Studies published by the Imre Nagy Institute for Political Research, Brussels, I (1959), 15.

NOTES TO CHAPTER FIVE

1. *Szabad Nép*, April 14, 1956.
2. Meray, *Thirteen Days*, p. 52.
3. See p. 31 above.
4. Later, in May, Rákosi under pressure acknowledged his personal guilt at a meeting of the Budapest Party "activists" (see Meray, *Thirteen Days*, pp. 284f.). This, too, failed to clear the air.
5. Personal interview.
6. Meray, *Thirteen Days*, p. 53.
7. Personal interview.
8. Personal interview.
9. Personal interview.
10. Meray, *Thirteen Days*, p. 55.   11. *Ibid.*, p. 58.
12. *Irodalmi Ujság*, June 30, 1956.

NOTES TO CHAPTER SIX

1. See pp. 78f. above.
2. See Coulter, "The Hungarian Peasantry: 1948–1956," *The American Slavic and East European Review*, XVIII (1959), 539–54.
3. See statistical table on "Development of Agricultural Socialization," in Helmreich (ed.), *Hungary*, pp. 238–39.
4. Personal interview.
5. Helmreich, *Hungary*, p. 241.
6. *Ibid.*   7. *Ibid.*, p. 242.   8. *Ibid.*, p. 382.

NOTES TO CHAPTER SEVEN

1. See p. 109 below.
2. Helmreich, *Hungary*, pp. 231f.

NOTES TO CHAPTER EIGHT

1. Meray, *Thirteen Days*, pp. 65f.
2. *Ibid.*, p. 69.   3. *Ibid.*, pp. 70f.
4. *Ibid.*, p. 80; Molnár and Nagy, *Imre Nagy, Réformateur ou Révolutionnaire?*, pp. 183f.
5. *Ibid.*, p. 188.
6. *A Magyar Forradalom és Szabadságharc* (The Hungarian Revolution and Struggle for Freedom), radio monitoring report [1956], p. 57.
7. This was imposed by Mikoyan, who flew to Budapest with Suslov on October 24 and stayed until the 26th. See Molnár and Nagy, *Imre Nagy*, pp. 193f.
8. *Ibid.*, pp. 197f.
9. "Hungarian Listeners to Western Broadcasts" (1957), p. 79.
10. See Lasky (ed.), *The Hungarian Revolution: A White Book*, pp. 169, 172.
11. In one of the bitterest and most lawless episodes of the revolution, the storming of the headquarters of the Budapest Party Organization in Republic Square on October 30, some non-AVH people were killed in battle or lynched afterward. One of the victims was Imre Mezö, Secretary of the Budapest Party Organization, a supporter of Nagy and the New Course. (See Meray, *Thirteen Days*, pp. 153f.)
12. "Hungarian Listeners to Western Broadcasts," p. 78.
13. On the workers' councils, see United Nations, *Report* (1957), paragraphs 542–61, pp. 91–94; also Oskar Anweiler, "Die Räte in der ungarischen Revolution 1956," *Ost-Europa*, VIII, No. 6 (1958), 393–400.
14. *A Magyar Forradalom*, pp. 61f.
15. Dr. Pavle Kovac, in *Deset godina nove Jugoslavije* (Ten Years of New Yugoslavia), quoted in *Ost-Probleme*, VIII, No. 51/52 (1956), 1795.
16. The following comment by Hannah Arendt is worth quoting in this connection: "Not the underprivileged, but the overprivileged of communist society took the initiative, and their motive was neither their own nor their fellow-citizens' material misery, but exclusively Freedom and Truth." ("Reflections on the Hungarian Revolution," *Journal of Politics*, XX [1958], 23.) The point is somewhat overstated, since concern about material misery in the mass did play a

part in the rebellion of the "overprivileged"; moreover, the under-privileged, too, seized the initiative when that became possible. The "overprivileged" acted first because they alone had an opportunity to act. Still, Arendt is right in pointing out the temporal priority of "elite" rebellion and the importance of moral factors in it.

NOTES TO CHAPTER NINE

1. The Czechoslovak information media made few references to the disorders. Details came from outside the country, from defectors' reports. The present account is based upon William E. Griffith, "Thaw and Frost in Eastern Europe," pp. 40–46 (manuscript), in which such reports are summarized.

2. Prior to the revolt, the numbers of people fleeing the East Zone for West Germany were as follows: 104,766 in 1950; 74,265 in 1951; and 150,218 in 1952. In 1953, the year of the revolt, the number shot up to 348,157. (*Statistisches Jahrbuch für die Bundesrepublik Deutschland,* 1958.)

3. The text in *Der Volksaufstand vom 17. Juni 1953, Denkschrift über den Juni-Aufstand in der sowjetischen Besatzungszone und in Ostberlin,* published by the Bundesministerium für gesamtdeutsche Fragen, Bonn, 1953, pp. 33f.

4. For reports from the East German press, see *ibid.,* pp. 25ff.

5. *SBZ von 1945 bis 1954,* published by the Federal Ministry for All-German Questions, Bonn, 1956, p. 239, as quoted in Carola Stern (pseud.), *Porträt einer bolschewistischen Partei,* Cologne, 1957, p. 154.

6. Stefan Brant (pseud.), *Der Aufstand, Vorgeschichte, Geschichte und Deutung des 17. Juni 1953,* Stuttgart, 1954, pp. 74ff.

7. For the full text of the resolution, see *Der Volksaufstand vom 17. Juni 1953,* pp. 35f.

8. Otto Lehmann, "Zu einigen schädlichen Erscheinungen bei der Erhöhung der Arbeitsnormen," *Tribüne (FDGB),* June 16, 1953; reprinted in *Der Volksaufstand vom 17. Juni,* pp. 43f.

9. For details of the revolutionary events, see Brant, *Der Aufstand; Der Volksaufstand vom 17. Juni;* and *Juni-Aufstand, Dokumente und Berichte über den Volksaufstand in Ostberlin und in der Sowjetzone,* published by the Federal Ministry for All-German Questions, Bonn, 1953.

10. Stern, *Porträt einer bolschewistischen Partei,* pp. 119ff.

11. *Ibid.,* pp. 163–67.

12. For events in Poland, see Georg W. Strobel, "Die nationale Komponente in der kommunistischen Entwicklung Polens," *Europa-Archiv,* XI, Nos. 22–23 (1956), 9317ff.; and Zbigniew K. Brzezinski,

The Soviet Bloc, Harvard University Press, Cambridge, Mass., 1960, Chapter 11.

13. See above, pp. 33ff.

14. K. S. Karol, *Visa for Poland,* London, 1959, p. 105.

15. *Ibid.,* pp. 109ff.

16. Stefan Korbonski, *Warsaw in Chains,* New York, 1959, pp. 282f. According to Karol (*Visa for Poland,* p. 116), "the date of his [Gomulka's] arrest is not known, but it was some time during 1950."

17. *Visa for Poland,* pp. 121ff.

18. Brzezinski, *The Soviet Bloc,* p. 238.

19. *Trybuna ludu,* January 27, 1955, quoted in Karol, *Visa for Poland,* p. 128.

20. Brzezinski, *The Soviet Bloc,* p. 240.

21. A detailed account of the Poznan uprising is found in Korbonski, *Warsaw in Chains,* pp. 284ff.

22. Brzezinski, *The Soviet Bloc,* pp. 251–54.

23. United Nations, *Report,* paragraph 226.

24. *Imre Nagy on Communism,* Chapter 3.

BIBLIOGRAPHY

Aczél, Tamás, and Király, Béla. "The Story Behind Hungary's Revolt," *Life*, February 18, 1957.
"The Aftermath of the Hungarian Revolution," *The World Today*, November 1957.
Arendt, Hannah. "Reflections on the Hungarian Revolution," *Journal of Politics*, Vol. XX, No. 1, February 1958.
Audience Analysis Section, Radio Free Europe, Munich. "Hungarian Listeners to Western Broadcasts." October 1957. Mimeographed.
"The Background of Hungary's Revolt," *Soviet Survey*, January 1957.
Bain, Leslie B. "How We Failed in Hungary," *The Reporter*, January 24, 1957.
Barber, Noël. A Handful of Ashes. London: Allan Wingate, 1957.
Beke, Laszlo. A Student's Diary. New York: The Viking Press, 1957.
Brzezinski, Zbigniew K. "U.S. Foreign Policy in East Central Europe—A Study in Contradictions," *Journal of International Affairs*, Vol. XI, No. 1, 1957.
———. The Soviet Bloc. Cambridge, Mass.: Harvard University Press, 1960.
Coulter, Harris L. "The Hungarian Peasantry: 1948–1956," *The American Slavic and East European Review*, Vol. XVIII, No. 4, December 1959.
"Les Débuts de la révolte des intellectuels," *Est et Ouest*, Vol. VIII, No. 164, December 16–31, 1956.
Delaney, Robert Finley (ed.). This Is Communist Hungary. Chicago: Regnery, 1958.
East Europe, December 1956, January 1957, July 1957. Special issues on the Hungarian Revolution.
Est et Ouest, Bulletin de l'Association d'Etudes et d'Informations Politiques Internationales (Paris). No. 181, October 16–31, 1957. Special issue on the Hungarian Revolution.
Fejtö, François. La Tragédie hongroise. Paris: Editions Pierre Horay, 1956.
———. Behind the Rape of Hungary. New York: David McKay Company, 1957.

Bibliography

Fossati, Luigi. Qui Budapest. Torino: Einaudi, 1957.

Fryer, Peter. Hungarian Tragedy. London: Dennis Dobson, 1956.

Galay, N. "The Lessons of the Hungarian Uprising," *Bulletin* of the Institute for the Study of the U.S.S.R., Munich, Vol. IV, No. 2, February 1957.

Garthoff, Raymond L. "The Tragedy of Hungary," *Problems of Communism*, Vol. VI, No. 1, January-February 1957.

Gasteyger, Curt. "Die Tragödie des ungarischen Volksaufstandes," *Europa-Archiv*, Vol. XI, Nos. 22 and 23, November 20 and December 5, 1956.

Gleitman, Henry, and Greenbaum, Joseph J. "Preliminary Results of Depth Interviews and Attitude Scales." New York: Free Europe Committee, n.d.

Gömöri, George. "Cultural and Literary Developments: Poland and Hungary," *The Annals of the American Academy of Political and Social Science*, Vol. CCCXVII, May 1958.

Healey, Denis (ed.). The Curtain Falls. London: Lincolns-Prager, 1951.

Helmreich, Ernst C. (ed.). Hungary. New York: published for the Mid-European Studies Center of the Free Europe Committee, Inc. by Frederick A. Praeger, 1957.

Hollo, Janos. "Youth vs. Communism: A Hungarian's Story," *The New York Times Weekly Magazine*, December 23, 1956.

"The Hungarian Revolution," *The World Today* (Royal Institute of International Affairs), January 1957.

"Hungary's Sacrifice," *Swiss Review of World Affairs* (Zurich), Vol. VI, No. 10, January 1957.

Ignotus, Paul. Political Prisoner. London: Routledge and Kegan Paul, 1959.

Imre Nagy on Communism. New York: Frederick A. Praeger, 1957.

International Commission of Jurists. "The Hungarian Situation and the Rule of Law." The Hague, April 1957.

———. "The Continuing Challenge of the Hungarian Situation to the Rule of Law." The Hague, June 1957. Supplement to the above.

International Research Associates. "Survey Among Hungarian Refugees in Austria." February 1957.

Kecskemeti, Paul. "Limits and Problems of Decompression: The Case of Hungary," *The Annals of the American Academy of Political and Social Science*, Vol. CCCXVII, May 1958.

Király, Béla. "How Russian Treachery Throttled Revolt," *Life*, February 18, 1957.

Kovago, Jozsef. You Are All Alone. New York: Frederick A. Praeger, 1959.

Lasky, Melvin J. (ed.). The Hungarian Revolution: A White Book.

Bibliography

New York: published for the Congress for Cultural Freedom by Frederick A. Praeger, 1957.

Listowel, Judith. "Hungary's Terrible Ordeal," *Saturday Evening Post*, January 5 and 12, 1957.

Madariaga, Salvador de. "Suez and Hungary," *Swiss Review of World Affairs* (Zurich), Vol. VI, No. 10, January 1957.

"A Magyar Forradalom és Szabadságharc a Hazai Rádióadások Tükrében, 1956 október 23–november 9, Magyarországi" (The Hungarian Revolution and Struggle for Freedom as Reflected in Domestic Radio Broadcasts, October 23–November 9, 1956, Hungarian Events). New York: Free Europe Press [1956]. A radio monitoring report.

"A Magyar Néphadsereg Szerepe" (Role of the Hungarian People's Army in the Revolution). New York: Free Europe Press, 1956.

Meray, Tibor. Thirteen Days That Shook the Kremlin: Imre Nagy and the Hungarian Revolution. New York: Frederick A. Praeger, 1959.

Mészáros, István. La Rivolta degli intellettuali in Ungheria. Milan: Giulio Einaudi, 1950.

Michener, James A. The Bridge at Andau. New York: Random House, 1957.

Mikes, George. The Hungarian Revolution. London: André Deutsch, 1957.

Molnár, Miklós, and Nagy, László. Imre Nagy, Réformateur ou Révolutionnaire? Geneva: Droz, and Paris: Minard, 1959.

Nagy, Ferenc. The Struggle Behind the Iron Curtain. New York: Macmillan, 1948.

Pfeiffer, Ede. Child of Communism. London: Weidenfeld and Nicolson, 1958.

"A rádió ostroma" (Siege of the Radio), *Népszabadság*, January 22, 1957.

"The Revolt in Hungary, A Documentary Chronology of Events, October 23, 1956–November 4, 1956." New York: Free Europe Committee, n.d.

Romanov, Al. "An Open Question," *Literaturnaya Gazeta* (English version in *Current Digest of the Soviet Press*, Vol. VIII, No. 47, January 2, 1957. Contains interviews with Hungarian writers).

Science and Freedom. No. 8, April 1957. Special issue on the Hungarian Revolution.

Silone, Ignazio. "Invitation à un Examen de Conscience," *L'Express*, Supplement to No. 285, December 7, 1956.

Stolte, Stefan C. "Moscow's Current Hungarian Policy," *Bulletin* of the Institute for the Study of the U.S.S.R., Munich, Vol. V, No. 7, July 1957.

Bibliography

Taylor, Edmond. "The Lessons of Hungary," *The Reporter*, December 27, 1956.

Les Temps Modernes (Paris). Vol. XII, Nos. 129, 130, and 131, November 1956, December 1956, January 1957. Special issues on the Hungarian Revolution.

United Nations. Report of the Special Committee on the Problem of Hungary. New York: 1957.

U.S. Congress, Committee on Foreign Affairs. "Report of the Special Study Mission to Europe on Policy toward the Satellite Nations." House Report No. 531, June 4, 1957.

Urban, George. The Nineteen Days. London: Heinemann, 1957.

Zinner, Paul E. (ed.). National Communism and Popular Revolt in Eastern Europe, A Selection of Documents. New York: Columbia University Press, 1956.

——. "Politics in East Central Europe," *Journal of International Affairs*, Vol. XI, No. 1, 1957.

——. "Revolution in Hungary: Reflections on the Vicissitudes of a Totalitarian System," *The Journal of Politics*, Vol. XXI, No. 1, 1959.

INDEX

Aczél, Tamás, 66–67, 68, 77, 107
Ady, Endre, 56
Age factor in Revolution, 112–14
Agriculture, Czech, 123
Agriculture, Hungarian: Nagy's position, 34–39, 44–46; collectivization, 38–39, 42–43, 88–91; workers shifted to industry, 41; Rákosi's position, 44–48 *passim*; land reform, 101–3; Communist controls, 103–5; *see also* Collectivization; Economy; Peasants
Agriculture, Ministry of, 15–16
Andopov, Yuri V., 78
Anti-Semitism, 29; *see also* Jews
Apro, Antal, 15
Arany, János, 56
"Atomization," 83–89

Batthyány, Count, 77
Béke és Szabadság ("Peace and Freedom"), 53
Benjámin, László, 59–60, 66f.
Beria, Lavrenti, 41–43, 48–49, 50, 134
Berman, Jacob, 135, 139
Bienkowski, Wladyslaw, 137
Bierut, Boleslaw, 135ff., 140
Budapest, University of, 12
Bulganin, Nikoli, 49–50

Classes: social, 92–105, 109–11;

cultural determinants of political behavior, 92–93; institutional determinants of political behavior, 93–94; disciplinary control, 95–99; *see also* "Atomization"; Intellectuals; Peasants; Students; Workers
Coalition government, 9–16; *see also* Hungary, government of
Collective Production, Ministry of, 36
Collectivization, 103–5, 122f., 125–29, 135–37; *see also* Agriculture; Economy; Peasants
Cominform, 26, 135–36
Communist parties, satellite: general discussion, 119–23, 149–59; Czech, 123–25; East German, 125–35; Polish, 135–48; *see also* Totalitarianism
Communist Party, Hungarian: postwar policies of, 4–6; postwar coalition government, 9–10; pre–World War II underground, 10–13; clash of Muscovites and indigenous underground in, 3, 13–16; terror against coalition partners, 17–18; intra-Party purges, 18–31; Nagy *vs.* Right opposition in, 32–39; Moscow introduces collective leadership in, 40–43; Nagy changes policies of,

173

Index

Index

lective Production, 36; Interior, 15–16
Molotov, Vladislav, 42, 141
Moral factor in Revolution, 3, 60–70, 117–18, 155–59
"Muscovites," the, 13–16 *passim*, 19–20
Müvelt Nép ("Cultured People"), 53

Nagy, Imre, 65, 68, 73; Minister of Agriculture, 15, 102; as leader of Right opposition, 32–39; becomes Premier, 4, 42–43; inaugurates New Course, 44–46; Rákosi sabotages New Course, 46–49; ousted by Rákosi from premiership, 49–52; supported by intellectuals, 67; opposes Gerö, 76–77; restored to Party membership, 78; halts collectivization drive, 90–91; opposition demands reinstatement of, 106–9; crowds clamor for, 111; workers' manifesto to, 114–15; personality, 144; role in intra-Party struggle, 145–51
National factor in Revolution, 80–81, 93–94, 117, 122–23, 147–48
Nemes, Dezsö, 34–37
Németh, László, 55
New Course, the 33–38, 40–54
Nowa kultura, 138
Nowak, Zenon, 142
"Nyirsegi Naplo" (Nyir County Diary), 64

Ochab, Edward, 140–42, 146

Pálfy-Oesterreicher, George, 15, 18, 25, 29n.
"Patriotic People's Front," 52
Patriotism, 93–94
"Peace Party," 13

Peasants, Czech, 123
Peasants, East German, 130
Peasants, Hungarian: alienated from Communist system, 4ff., 11; and the New Course, 33–38, 43–48, 130; and collectivization, 38–41; as theme in new writing, 64–65; resistance to Communist control, 88–91; reforms for, 15, 101–5; revolutionary activity, 109–10; revolutionary motivation of, 117; *see also* Classes; Economy
Peasants Party, 13–14
"People's Front of Independence," 17–18
Periodicals, 53, 65
Péter, Gábor, 15, 31
Petöfi Circle Committee, 53, 70, 72–73, 76; *see also* Intellectuals, Hungarian
Petöfi, Sándor, 56
Plzen uprising, 123–25, 134
Poland, 8, 116, 135–48
Police, political (AVH), 5f., 15, 26–28, 31, 45, 73–77, 94, 112
Po prostu, 138
Popular Front, 12
Poznan uprising, 73, 75, 78, 146
Purges, Hungarian intra-Party, 18–31; general discussion, 18–20; "opposition" hypothesis, 21–24; "rivalry" hypothesis, 25–28; "loyalty" hypothesis, 28–31

Rajk, Julia, 74, 77
Rajk, László: as leader of indigenous underground, 12–15 *passim*, 19–20; Minister of the Interior, 16; career declines, 17–18; expulsion and execution of, 18–19; hypotheses to explain purge of, 19–20; "opposition" hypothesis, 21–24; "rivalry" hypothesis, 25–

Index

Index

OTHER VOLUMES OF

RAND RESEARCH

THE UNIVERSITY OF CHICAGO PRESS, CHICAGO, ILLINOIS:
Water Supply: Economics, Technology, and Policy
  Jack Hirshleifer, James C. DeHaven, and Jerome W. Milliman,
  1960

COLUMBIA UNIVERSITY PRESS, NEW YORK:
Soviet National Income and Product, 1940–48
  Abram Bergson and Hans Heymann, Jr., 1954
Soviet National Income and Product in 1928
  Oleg Hoeffding, 1954
Labor Productivity in Soviet and American Industry
  Walter Galenson, 1955

THE FREE PRESS, GLENCOE, ILLINOIS:
Psychosis and Civilization
  Herbert Goldhamer and Andrew W. Marshall, 1953
Soviet Military Doctrine
  Raymond L. Garthoff, 1953
A Study of Bolshevism
  Nathan Leites, 1953
Ritual of Liquidation: The Case of the Moscow Trials
  Nathan Leites and Elsa Bernaut, 1954
*Two Studies in Soviet Controls: Communism and the Russian Peas-
  ant, and Moscow in Crisis*
  Herbert S. Dinerstein and Leon Gouré, 1955
A Million Random Digits with 100,000 Normal Deviates
  The RAND Corporation, 1955

HARVARD UNIVERSITY PRESS, CAMBRIDGE, MASSACHUSETTS:
Smolensk under Soviet Rule
    Merle Fainsod, 1958
The Economics of Defense in the Nuclear Age
    Charles J. Hitch and Roland McKean, 1960

THE MACMILLAN COMPANY, NEW YORK:
China Crosses the Yalu: The Decision To Enter the Korean War
    Allen S. Whiting, 1960
Protective Construction in a Nuclear Age
    Edited by J. J. O'Sullivan, 1961

MCGRAW-HILL BOOK COMPANY, INC., NEW YORK:
The Operational Code of the Politburo
    Nathan Leites, 1951
*Air War and Emotional Stress: Psychological Studies of Bombing
    and Civilian Defense*
    Irving L. Janis, 1951
*Soviet Attitudes Toward Authority: An Interdisciplinary Approach
    to Problems of Soviet Character*
    Margaret Mead, 1951
Mobilizing Resources for War: The Economic Alternatives
    Tibor Scitovsky, Edward Shaw, and Lorie Tarshis, 1951
*The Organizational Weapon: A Study of Bolshevik Strategy and
    Tactics*
    Philip Selznick, 1952
Introduction to the Theory of Games
    J. C. C. McKinsey, 1952
Weight-Strength Analysis of Aircraft Structures
    F. R. Shanley, 1952
*The Compleat Strategyst: Being a Primer on the Theory of Games
    of Strategy*
    J. D. Williams, 1954
Linear Programming and Economic Analysis
    Robert Dorfman, Paul A. Samuelson, and Robert M. Solow, 1958
Introduction to Matrix Analysis
    Richard Bellman, 1960
The Theory of Linear Economic Models
    David Gale, 1960

THE MICROCARD FOUNDATION, MADISON, WISCONSIN:
The First Six Million Prime Numbers
    C. L. Baker and F. J. Gruenberger, 1959

NORTH-HOLLAND PUBLISHING COMPANY, AMSTERDAM, HOLLAND:
A Time Series Analysis of Interindustry Demands
Kenneth J. Arrow and Marvin Hoffenberg, 1959

FREDERICK A. PRAEGER, PUBLISHERS, NEW YORK:
*War and the Soviet Union: Nuclear Weapons and the Revolution
in Soviet Military and Political Thinking*
H. S. Dinerstein, 1959

PRENTICE-HALL, INC., ENGLEWOOD CLIFFS, NEW JERSEY:
Games of Strategy: Theory and Applications
Melvin Dresher, 1961

PRINCETON UNIVERSITY PRESS, PRINCETON, NEW JERSEY:
Approximations for Digital Computers
Cecil Hastings, Jr., 1955
*International Communication and Political Opinion: A Guide to the
Literature*
Bruce Lannes Smith and Chitra M. Smith, 1956
Dynamic Programming
Richard Bellman, 1957
The Berlin Blockade: A Study in Cold War Politics
W. Phillips Davison, 1958
The French Economy and the State
Warren C. Baum, 1958
Strategy in the Missile Age
Bernard Brodie, 1959
Foreign Aid: Theory and Practice in Southern Asia
Charles Wolf, Jr., 1960
Adaptive Control Processes: A Guided Tour
Richard Bellman, 1961

PUBLIC AFFAIRS PRESS, WASHINGTON, D.C.:
The Rise of Khrushchev
Myron Rush, 1958
Behind the Sputniks: A Survey of Soviet Space Science
F. J. Krieger, 1958

RANDOM HOUSE, INC., NEW YORK:
Space Handbook: Astronautics and Its Applications
Robert W. Buchheim and the Staff of The RAND Corporation,
1959

ROW, PETERSON AND COMPANY, EVANSTON, ILLINOIS:

German Rearmament and Atomic War: The Views of German Military and Political Leaders
Hans Speier, 1957

West German Leadership and Foreign Policy
Edited by Hans Speier and W. Phillips Davison, 1957

The House without Windows: France Selects a President
Constantin Melnik and Nathan Leites, 1958

Propaganda Analysis: A Study of Inferences Made from Nazi Propaganda in World War II
Alexander L. George, 1959

STANFORD UNIVERSITY PRESS, STANFORD, CALIFORNIA:

Strategic Surrender: The Politics of Victory and Defeat
Paul Kecskemeti, 1958

On the Game of Politics in France
Nathan Leites, 1959

Atomic Energy in the Soviet Union
Arnold Kramish, 1959

Marxism in Southeast Asia: A Study of Four Countries
Edited by Frank N. Trager, 1959

JOHN WILEY & SONS, INC., NEW YORK:

Efficiency in Government through Systems Analysis: With Emphasis on Water Resource Development
Roland N. McKean, 1958